AT HEAVEN'S EDGE

ANDREA JO RODGERS

HARVEST HOUSE PUBLISHERS
EUGENE, OREGON

Scripture quotations are taken from the Holy Bible, New International Version®, NIV®. Copyright © 1973, 1978, 1984, 2011 by Biblica, Inc.® Used by permission. All rights reserved worldwide.

Cover by Writely Designed, Enumclaw, Washington

Cover photo © CandyBoxImages / PhotoDune

Names and minor details have been changed in the real-life stories shared in this book to protect the privacy of the individuals mentioned.

AT HEAVEN'S EDGE

Published by Harvest House Publishers
Eugene, Oregon 97402
www.harvesthousepublishers.com

Library of Congress Cataloging-in-Publication Data
    Rodgers, Andrea, 1970-
    At heaven's edge / Andrea Rodgers.
        pages cm
    ISBN 978-0-7369-6459-3 (pbk.)
    ISBN 978-0-7369-6460-9 (eBook)
    1. Emergency medical services—Anecdotes. 2. Rodgers, Andrea, 1970—Anecdotes. 3. Rodg-
    ers, Andrea, 1970—Religion. 4. Emergency medical technicians—United States—Anecdotes.
    5. Near-death experiences—Religious aspects—Christianity—Anecdotes. 6. Accident victims—
    United States—Anecdotes. I Title.
    RA645.5.R64A3 2015
    616.02'5—dc23
                                                                                    2014038260

Printed in the United States of America

18 19 20 21 22 23 / BP-JH / 10 9 8 7 6 5 4

Dedicated to
the loving memory of my parents,
Andrew and Annemarie.

Acknowledgments

A special thanks to my husband, Rick, my sister, Thea, and my friends Katy and Colleen for their time and encouragement. Thanks to Reverend David Cotton and Bishop David O'Connell for their support and prayers, and to my literary agent, Leslie Stobbe, for his wisdom and guidance. Also, thank you to the staff at Harvest House Publishers and especially my editor, Kathleen Kerr, for her professional assistance.

Contents

Preface

911 emergencies catch us at our most vulnerable. In our darkest, most frightening moments, when we are forced to face our mortality head-on, many of us turn to the Lord. In these times of crisis, He hears our pleas for help. Sometimes, the assistance may be a direct intervention from God. Other times, He may help us indirectly through the efforts of first responders. During these times, the volunteer EMS community is blessed to be able to serve as instruments of Jesus. In these moments of despair, we often unexpectedly find inspiration.

The Elevator Accident

Be strong and courageous. Do not be afraid or
terrified because of them, for the LORD your God goes
with you; he will never leave you nor forsake you.
DEUTERONOMY 31:6

The force of the crash nearly knocked my young son, John, and me off our feet. The elevator jerked violently and I grabbed for the wall to steady myself. A loud noise, reminiscent of the time I rode on the Maid of the Mist at Niagara Falls, filled the air. *But why in the world am I hearing the sound of gushing water?* I felt my heart begin to thump unnaturally in my chest and instinctively tightened my grip on John's hand.

It was ten o'clock in the morning on a beautiful October day—my seventh wedding anniversary, to be exact. Outside, the warm early autumn sun kissed the colorful golden and crimson leaves. In sharp contrast to the outdoors, the elevator was quickly morphing into a chamber of terrors for John and me.

The morning started with an ordinary visit to John's eye doctor, Dr. Mendel. John, a two-year-old toddler, had gotten glasses six weeks earlier because he is farsighted. Today was a follow-up visit to see how he was doing. The visit didn't take more than a half hour. The receptionist, Louise, handed me an appointment card on my way out. "We'll see John again in four weeks, Mrs. Rodgers."

Smiling, I put the card in my pocket and waved goodbye. I was already planning the rest of my day off: picnicking at the playground by our home, reading together at the library, apple picking at a local farm. Later that evening, my husband, Rick, and I wanted to rewatch our wedding video, one of our favorite anniversary traditions. *This is going to be a picture-perfect anniversary.*

When we stepped out into the hallway, I decided on the spur of the moment to take the elevator. Usually I prefer the stairs, but I figured an elevator ride would be a fun adventure for John. Just like most toddlers, he was eager to discover new and exciting things.

"Do you want to take the elevator?" I asked him, although I already knew what his answer would be.

"Yes, yes," John answered, a 1000-megawatt smile lighting up his trusting face. Wriggling with excitement, he rushed ahead into the elevator.

"Press the button with the *one* on it," I said to him, holding his small hand in my own.

"One," John said softly, pressing the button with me.

Somewhere in the back of my mind, it dimly registered that the ride seemed to be taking a little bit longer than it should have. I brushed the thought aside. But within seconds, the elevator crashed and made a terrifying grinding metallic noise unlike anything I had ever heard before in my life. A sick feeling erupted in the pit of my stomach. *What's going on? What's happening to us? I want to get out now!*

Suddenly, I realized why the noise I was hearing sounded like running water. It *was* running water! To my horror, it began rushing under the bottom of the elevator door with a vengeance. *I absolutely cannot believe this is happening to us!*

For a split second, I stared in shocked disbelief. Then my brain clicked into gear and I hoisted John into my arms as the water rushed up and over his ankles. I frantically pressed the *door open* button a dozen times. When that didn't work, I began pushing at the door in a desperate attempt to open it. *Help me, Lord. Tell me what to do! Please get us out of here!*

Have you ever had an experience that lasts a few moments but seems to go on for a lifetime? When your mind desperately tries to grasp exactly what is going on?

I began screaming, but the scream sounded oddly disconnected from my body. My mind flashed to Rick. He is my rock, my true love, my best friend. Next, my mind swept to my sweet daughter, Anna. *Will I ever see them again?*

The water quickly rose above my knees. At that moment, I was forced to face my mortality. My heart was thumping so hard in my chest that I felt like it could explode at any moment. *Are we going to die? I don't want to die. I'm not ready to die! We're both too young to die! Dear Lord, please save us!*

John's terrified silence stood in stark contrast to my screams for help. The water continued rising higher and higher. If I hadn't lifted John up, the water would now be over his head. *If the water keeps coming in, will we float up to the ceiling? Will we be able to get out that way? Will I be able to tread water while holding on to John? Or will we both go under? Are we going to drown?*

I've been a volunteer on my town's first aid squad for 26 years and have answered over 6500 calls for help. This was the very first time that the tables were turned. Rather than responding to a 911 emergency, I *was* the 911 emergency.

Water continued to rush underneath the elevator doors. I pressed the alarm button over and over again but didn't hear any sort of audible alarm. *Is the button working? Does anyone know that John and I are trapped in this elevator?*

"Help!" I screamed as loudly as I could. *I don't want to die in this elevator! I don't want my husband to be a widower! I don't want my daughter to grow up without John and me!* But as the water continued to rise, I feared that John and I would surely drown.

And then, in that incredibly dark moment, God answered my prayer. Miraculously, the elevator doors slowly opened! *Our guardian angels are working overtime to rescue us!*

With John still in my arms, I staggered out of the elevator into a dark basement filled with water. I could hear water running all around us, the sound echoing eerily off the cement walls. Dim light filtered through a small basement window. Across the room, I thought I could make out the outline of a door. *Please, please let that be a way out of here!*

I was crying so hard that it made it even harder to see. Clutching John tightly to me, I waded through the water. I yanked the door open and, to my relief, saw a flight of stairs directly in front of me. I staggered up the stairs, sobbing uncontrollably. At the time John weighed about 35 pounds, but there was no way I was going to let go of my precious child. I clung to him as though he was my life preserver.

John, in sharp contrast to me, was ominously silent. His tiny arms clung around my neck. His eyes were wide open, fear reflecting in their depths. I wanted to tell him that everything would be okay, but I couldn't get any words out. *Jesus saved us. We're going to live!*

I was crying so hard that I missed the door to the first floor. I opened the first door that I saw and stepped out into a hallway. After a moment, I realized that I was back on the second floor again.

Almost in a daze, I worked my way back to Dr. Mendel's office. As I entered the waiting room, I was sobbing so much that I couldn't speak. I was trembling all over but couldn't seem to stop myself. *Try to get a grip on yourself, girl! You're okay! You're both safe! You're out of the elevator!*

Louise, the receptionist, rushed out from behind her desk to help me. "Mrs. Rodgers, what's wrong?" she asked. She knew I had left a mere ten minutes ago with a cheery goodbye. Now suddenly I was back, sobbing for some unknown reason.

"The elevator," I managed to say.

The rest of the office staff came out from behind the counter and crowded around me. Louise led me to a seat. "Stay right here. I'm going to get Dr. Mendel."

A few seconds later, Dr. Mendel came to my side. "Call 911," he directed Louise. "Tell them we need the fire department and first aid squad right away."

A young man holding a baby in an infant carrier stepped forward. "I already did. When I was downstairs, I was trying to get into the elevator. I heard your screams but I couldn't tell where they were coming from. I went into one of the offices down there and told them to call 911."

Louise kindly brought John and me glasses of water. I tried to stop crying so I could explain what had happened. I knew I was frightening John. He stared at me with his big blue eyes and said not a word.

The fire department and emergency medical technicians arrived a few minutes later. *I can't believe that they are here for me! It's usually the other way around!*

"The fire chief is checking the basement and the elevator," Louise said. "Just sit right here and rest, sweetie."

Several minutes later, the fire chief returned. "We're going to have to evacuate this entire building," he said. "It's going to need to be closed for the rest of the day. We have a very severe electrical hazard in the basement."

A severe electrical hazard in the basement! I had thought John and I were going to drown. It hadn't even occurred to me that we were nearly electrocuted. I had walked through that electrical hazard! I had waded through that deep water with little John in my arms! And by the grace of God we didn't "fry." By the grace of God we lived! I cried even harder. But this time, they were tears of relief rather than terror. And in that moment, I knew in my heart of hearts that John and I were not alone in that elevator. Jesus was with us the whole time.

During the accident, I injured my neck, back, and knee. Afterward, I was plagued by flashbacks and an uneasy feeling. I had trouble concentrating and was worried because I was in a doctoral program. I needed to be able to concentrate to do well in my classes. I also developed a fear of enclosed spaces. I knew I needed help.

John started having nightmares; he would wake up screaming "Mommy!" For many months, he would say, "The elevator had water and Mommy cried." Upon our pastor's recommendation, John and I both went to a social worker specializing in Christian-focused counseling. These sessions helped start the healing process.

Over the following weeks, I began to pull myself together as I experienced the loving and healing presence of Jesus through the outpouring of love and support from friends and family. About a week after the accident, I arrived home from work and discovered a gift bag on our front porch. Inside was a beautiful wall hanging decorated with Easter lilies. It read, "If God brings you to it, He will bring you through it." There was no card or clue with the gift to indicate who it might be from. Several days later, I learned it was from the ten-year-old daughter of a coworker. Her mother had told her the story about our accident, and the child was so moved that she told her mother she wanted to buy us a present. The words on the plaque and the thoughtfulness behind the gift brought me immeasurable comfort. The present continues to hold a special place of honor on our dining room wall.

I began answering first aid calls as a volunteer emergency medical technician with my local rescue squad again. At first, it brought tears of pain to my eyes to carry the heavy first aid bag. It was difficult to climb stairs and to kneel down next to patients because my knee kept buckling. But I persevered. I refused to give in to the pain and, through prayer and God's grace, I was able to move on. *Thank You, Lord, for walking beside me.*

Answering first aid calls helped me take the focus off my own problems and redirect it onto someone else. It was a balm to my soul to know that I was doing something positive instead of just focusing on the negative.

I am forever grateful that John and I lived that day. The good Lord gave John and me a second chance by helping us to miraculously survive the elevator accident. Thank You, Jesus, for answering my cry for help and for allowing me to experience firsthand Your loving and healing presence in my life.

Buried Alive!

He performs wonders that cannot be fathomed,
miracles that cannot be counted.

JOB 5:9

This is the best day ever! Morgan Zuckerman arrived at the beach early in the morning with her grandfather. Morgan's parents were away for a long weekend, so she was spending three days with her grandpa. On Saturday, the pair spent the day at an amusement park. Sunday, they went to a movie and then ate dinner at Morgan's favorite restaurant. Now today, Grandpa promised they could spend the entire day at the beach.

Morgan paused to take a rest from shoveling sand. *This is going to be the biggest, best hole in the whole world!* Morgan studied her handiwork. So far, the hole was about three feet wide, three feet long, and five feet deep. *Another foot should do the trick!* Humming her favorite tune, Morgan resumed shoveling.

A half hour later or so, Morgan took another rest. Now the hole was so deep, she could no longer see the volleyball players who were playing a short distance away. But she could still hear their occasional yells and cheers when someone scored a point. *Maybe I'll climb out for a little while and ask Grandpa if we can go to the snack stand and get an ice cream cone.*

Morgan reached up toward the top of the hole, but her fingers fell about six inches short. *Wow—it's even deeper than I thought! I guess I can just climb out using my legs.* Morgan carefully dug one foot in the sandy

15

wall and then reached up toward the top. To her dismay, her foot slid down and a bit of sand came with it.

I hope when I climb out I don't mess up my hole. Once more, Morgan dug her right foot into the wall and stretched up with her hands. But once again, her foot slid back down with a small pile of sand landing on top of it.

Oh, well. I want to get out and get that ice cream. If some sand caves in, I can always dig it out again later. This time, Morgan dug her foot in more vigorously and jumped up toward the top of the hole. But it was no use. Morgan landed back down at the bottom of the hole. Again.

"Grandpa?" Morgan said tentatively. But Grandpa did not reply. Now Morgan found herself wishing that she had dug the hole closer to where her grandfather was sitting. She felt the beginnings of fear stir deep in the pit of her tummy. *What if I can't get out? Should I yell for help? Will Grandpa hear me? Or will the volleyball players hear me? Maybe I should try jumping one more time...*

With a mighty heave, Morgan leaped up toward the top of the hole. Sand began raining down on her in a torrent. Morgan tried to scream, but her mouth quickly filled up with sand.

Panic and terror consumed her. *I can't see anything! I can't hear anything! How will I ever get out of here?* Morgan Zuckerman had been buried alive!

....

The volleyball sailed high over Martha Frederick's head.

"Hey," her friend Jed said. "Are you daydreaming out there?"

"Sorry," Martha laughed. "I'll go get it!" *I guess I was daydreaming...thinking about how nice it is to play volleyball again with all my old college friends.* Wiping sweat from her forehead, she turned and began jogging along the sand toward where the ball landed.

When Martha reached the ball, she froze. Something didn't feel quite right. Something was different. And then she realized...the hole the little girl had been digging all morning was gone! But where was the girl? Had she gotten bored and filled the hole back in? Had she gone home for the day?

Martha glanced around. She spotted the little girl's relative, an older man with short gray hair, standing about twenty feet away. She noticed a pair of empty beach chairs close beside him. She assumed the man was the child's grandfather. Martha got a funny feeling...

Jed jogged up beside Martha. "What's wrong?" he asked. "Did you turn into a sand sculpture? You seem frozen to the spot," he joked.

"Do you remember seeing that girl digging the hole?" Martha asked.

"Of course," Jed replied. He turned toward where the hole used to be, and a shadow crossed his face. "Martha, you don't think that..."

"I don't know. I'm going over and asking her grandfather where she is."

"I'll go with you," Jed offered.

The pair approached Morgan's grandfather, Mr. Zuckerman. "Excuse me," Martha began. "This may seem like a really strange question, but where is the little girl who was with you earlier? The one who was digging that big hole."

"I was just looking for her. I saw her about four or five minutes ago, but now I can't seem to see her. She was right over there," Mr. Zuckerman said, pointing toward the area where the hole used to be. "Have you seen her?"

"No, I'm afraid not," Jed said. "And the hole is gone."

"Do you think she may have gone up to the bathroom or to the water fountain?" Mr. Zuckerman asked, concern evident on his face.

"I don't know. Wouldn't she have told you she was going?" Martha asked. It still didn't feel right to her.

"Well, not necessarily. I'm not sure," Mr. Zuckerman said slowly, the full horrible insinuation of what Martha and Jed were hinting at starting to dawn on him. "She couldn't possibly be..."

"When did you say was the last time you saw her?" Martha asked.

"I'm not exactly sure. Maybe four or five minutes ago," Mr. Zuckerman, now visibly frightened, replied.

Martha and Jed exchanged looks. "Jed, notify the lifeguards and tell them to call 911!"

"I'm on it," he answered, already running toward the lifeguard stand.

Martha ran over to the approximate area where she had seen Morgan digging the hole. *I wish I had paid more attention to exactly where she was digging.* She estimated the hole could have been anywhere in about a fifteen-foot radius.

Martha waved for her volleyball friends to come over. "Listen, I think there may be a young girl under the sand somewhere around here," she said, her voice catching with emotion. "We need to start digging."

Martha didn't have to say another word. Her friends had also seen the child digging and now put two and two together. They frantically began digging in the hot sand with their bare hands.

"Jed's getting the lifeguards," Martha said. "Let's hope we find her right away!" *Is she even under the sand? Could she have gone down to the bathroom like her grandfather suggested? And if she is under the sand, is it futile? Will we ever find her? And if we do, will she still be alive?*

. . . .

It was a typical hot and sunny summer day. The beach was packed with sun worshippers who were trying to beat the heat. At the time, I was working as a special officer (better known as a beach cop). I spent the morning checking beach badges, responding to a first aid call for a fall victim, and picking a boardwalk splinter out of a teenage boy's big toe. Nothing too exciting. I had just returned from my lunch break and was riding my police bike along the boardwalk when my first aid pager beeped.

> **DISPATCHER:** "First aid requested at the Shelton Avenue Beach for a girl buried alive."

What? Buried alive? Did I just hear that correctly? I was only one block away from the location of the call. Swerving around numerous pedestrians, I began biking as fast as I could.

When I reached Shelton Avenue, I quickly ditched my bike and jumped the boardwalk railing onto the beach. A small crowd was forming about thirty feet past the boardwalk, behind the lifeguard stand. I could see that several lifeguards and a group of volleyball players were digging frantically.

I spotted Officer Vinnie McGovern in the midst of the group of people. Officer McGovern had been on the police force for about a dozen years. I edged my way through the crowd to him.

"Andrea, we may have a young girl under here somewhere. Start digging!" he said.

I joined in and started clawing at the sand as fast as I could. But I quickly realized that as fast as we dug the sand, some of it would slide right back again. I could feel my heart beginning to thump unnaturally hard in my chest. *This is a total nightmare. We need help, Lord!*

As I dug, I caught snatches of conversations going on around me.

"She dug a six-foot hole. I heard she was digging it all day…"

"One of the volleyball players noticed the hole wasn't there anymore…"

"Her grandfather said he's hoping she just wandered off to the bathroom, but he isn't sure where she is…"

"We started digging where we saw her digging earlier today…"

"Someone is running down to the bathroom to look for her…"

"We figured we better start digging just in case…"

"We think the hole was around here somewhere, but we're not exactly sure…"

"She's only twelve years old…"

"Her name is Morgan…"

It was quickly turning into a mob scene. More people joined in the digging. I was glad to see a few of them had shovels. *Morgan, where are you? Will we ever find you?*

"Someone just got back from checking the bathroom. She's not in there," one of the lifeguards said. "We need to keep digging!"

The girl's grandfather stood close by. His face was ashen and he looked as though he might faint. A kindly bystander tried to comfort him. *I can't imagine what must be running through that poor man's head. What will he say to Morgan's parents if he comes home without their daughter?*

One minute…two minutes…three minutes…With each minute that ticked by, I knew the risk of Morgan sustaining brain damage grew. *Dear Lord, we need to find her!*

The hole gradually grew bigger, but there was still no sign of Morgan. More and more people joined in to help. Several of the lifeguards called out directions to better organize the effort.

We dug and dug. My arms burned. My eyes stung. My adrenalin surged. *We need to find Morgan. And we need to do it really fast.*

I could hear people crying behind me. I didn't look at them. I focused on one thing: digging. The people close around me did the same thing. And as I dug, I sent up a silent prayer that we would find Morgan. *Alive.*

Four minutes…five minutes passed. We kept digging.

"I think I see something! I think I see hair!" a man two feet in front of me shouted. Our digging efforts zeroed in on the spot where the man pointed.

I squinted in the sunlight. The man was correct; I could see that there was definitely something there in the sand. *Dear God, please let it be Morgan!*

First, I saw some dark brown hair emerge. Then a forehead, nose, mouth, and a chin. By the grace of God, we had found her!

Morgan's eyes were closed and her face was completely blue. Officer McGovern opened her mouth to try to open her airway, but her mouth was filled with sand. A lifeguard held Morgan's head steady while Officer McGovern scooped the sand out of her mouth. I could clearly see that she was unconscious, but I wasn't sure whether or not she had a pulse. *Is she alive? Will she make it? Can she survive?*

Several of us kept carefully digging to free the rest of Morgan's body. One of our members, Colleen Harper, held an oxygen mask to Morgan's face. I marveled at how Morgan's small body was absolutely vertical in the sand. It appeared as though she had been literally buried alive. The six-foot hole she had dug must have suddenly caved in on her while she was standing in it.

The crowd buzzed with excitement as word spread. "We've found her! We've found her!"

After we finished digging Morgan out, we carefully hoisted her up out of the hole. Suddenly, her eyes snapped open and she took a big breath. *She's alive!*

Morgan blinked, her eyes glazed with confusion. Coughing, she reached toward her mouth to brush out more sand.

"Oh, my precious child. Oh, my beautiful Morgan," her grandfather sobbed, kneeling down next to her. "I love you so much!" Tears of relief streamed down his face.

Morgan nodded her head and reached toward Grandpa. The two embraced, rocking back and forth as they tightly hugged each other. "Time to take you to the hospital to get checked out, sweetie," he said gently.

We transferred Morgan onto a backboard and carried her off the beach to our first aid stretcher, which was set up on the boardwalk. As we walked by, the crowd of bystanders clapped and cheered wildly.

I knew Morgan wasn't totally out of the woods. I realized that she may have aspirated sand into her lungs, which could cause complications such as pneumonia. There was also a risk that she may have suffered an anoxic brain injury. But for now, I rejoiced that she was alive!

On that day, God acted through many people, including volleyball players, police, EMS, lifeguards, and bystanders to miraculously rescue Morgan. That day stands out in my memory as one in which many people joined together to form a patchwork team that quickly formed a cohesive unit. A cohesive unit that, with the divine intervention of the Lord, saved the life of a little girl.

Morgan made a full recovery. She did not suffer any ill consequences and was released from the hospital the next day. A true miracle!

Our Heroic Men in Blue

He will bring you a message through which
you and all your household will be saved.

ACTS 11:14

"Just one more bag to bring in, honey," Perry Parker called to his wife, Madeline, from the garage. They had just finished their weekly trip to the grocery store. As was their tradition, Perry carried in the grocery bags, and Madeline unpacked them and put the food away.

"Thanks, dear," she responded absentmindedly. She was trying to figure out what to cook for dinner. Madeline was pushing eighty and starting to feel it. She wasn't really in the mood to cook and now found herself wishing they had grabbed some fast food on the way home. She just wanted to put her feet up and rest for a bit.

Soup. Yes, soup and a nice, warm loaf of fresh bread. That will do the trick. Madeline pulled a few cans out of an oak kitchen cabinet and turned on the gas stovetop. *The soup will be warm by the time I finish unpacking.*

Perry came in with the last bag and placed it on the counter. "Do you need any help?" he lovingly asked his wife of fifty years. "You look a bit under the weather."

"Sure, thanks. Just a bit tired. It's not as easy as it used to be," she replied, leaning against the kitchen counter for support. It was a conversation they'd had numerous times over the past few years. Lapsing into a comfortable silence, they finished preparing the meal and sat down at the kitchen table.

Madeline glanced at her watch. "*Jeopardy* starts in fifteen minutes," she said. They never missed it. Madeline and Perry moved to their recliners in the living room, as was their custom. *Ah, now I can finally rest.*

During a commercial break, Madeline turned towards Perry. "Honey, I really don't feel so hot. My head hurts and I feel kind of weak." She couldn't put a finger on it, but something just didn't feel quite right.

Perry turned to her with concern. "What's going on, sweetie?" He tried to get up and go over to his wife but suddenly realized that he couldn't. His legs simply refused to cooperate.

Slowly, Madeline's eyes grew blurry, so she closed them. She tried to answer her husband but found that she couldn't. *Something's terribly wrong! What's happening to me? Why can't I talk anymore?*

"Madeline? Madeline? Speak to me. What's wrong?" Perry asked with growing alarm. But Madeline remained quiet, for she had lapsed into unconsciousness. Perry made another attempt to get up and help his wife, but it was no use. And now, he found that he could barely move his arms. With every last bit of his strength, he reached for the phone and dialed 911.

"Pine Cove Police. What is your emergency?" dispatcher Jerome Franklin asked. Jerome had been with the Pine Cove Police Department for the better part of ten years. He was uniformly respected by all the officers for his knowledge, efficiency, and dedication.

"My wife," Perry said weakly. Even his voice was threatening to quit. He tried to rally his strength. He knew that he needed to get Madeline help right away.

"Sir? Where do you live? What's wrong with your wife?" Jerome questioned, his full attention focused on the caller.

"Help," Perry said feebly.

"Speak to me, sir. Tell me what's happening," Jerome urged.

The phone line grew silent. Jerome looked at the caller ID and quickly did a reverse lookup. He knew that he needed to dispatch the police and first aid immediately.

....

It was a cold and blustery Tuesday evening in early February. Earlier, my mom made one of my favorites, stuffed peppers, for dinner. At that moment, as I was enjoying quality time with my family, another family in town was struggling to survive.

DISPATCHER: "First aid requested at 608 Chambers Road for an unknown nature: possibly two people falling unconscious."

My mom, who was sitting next to me, heard the dispatcher. "Two falling unconscious at the same time?"

"Yes, it sounds a bit strange, doesn't it?" I replied as I threw on my winter coat and headed out. Occasionally we will have two calls in one home at the same time, but it is fairly rare. For example, one person falls and another gets injured trying to catch them. Or they both have stomach bugs or food poisoning.

Officers Fred Smith and Jim Jones arrived at the Parkers' home in record time. Whereas Fred was approaching retirement, Jim was a rookie with the department. They made a great team.

Fred and Jim raced up the front porch steps. "I'm not sure what we've got, Jim," Fred said as he tried the front door. "Locked!"

Jim tried the front window, but it was also locked. "Do you think we should…"

"Yeah," Fred said. "Make sure you hold your breath. On the count of three…" Shoulder to shoulder, the two strong men broke the front door down.

With relief, Mr. Parker watched as Officers Smith and Jones entered his home. He recalled many years ago, when Fred Smith was a young boy just learning how to fish. Now, here he was, ready to help them. And yet, when Mr. Parker tried to tell them what was wrong, no words would come out. He wanted to point to Madeline, but his arm wouldn't budge. He could barely keep his eyes open…

Officer Smith dared not open his mouth to speak, fearful that something was amiss in the house and that he might breathe in some unknown poison. Instead, he tapped Officer Jones on the shoulder and pointed to Mrs. Parker. Then he gestured that he would take care of Mr. Parker. Seamlessly, they worked as a team. While Officer Jones hoisted Madeline over his shoulders, Officer Smith did the same with her husband. Together, in a race against the clock, they rushed outside into the fresh air. Realizing it was too frigid to stay outdoors, Officer Smith, still carrying Mr. Parker, banged on a neighbor's front door. "Pine Cove Police! This is an emergency! Open the door!" Fred shouted.

Mrs. Donaldson, already in her pink terrycloth house robe and with light blue curlers in her hair, was just about to go upstairs to watch television with her husband. In shock, she threw open her front door and gasped in horror at the sight of her beloved neighbors, seemingly unconscious in the arms of two police officers. "Come in, come in," she said, her voice shaking. To her husband, she called, "Bennie, come quick! It's the Parkers!"

Officer Smith, staggering from the weight of Mr. Parker, carried him across the threshold. Bennie Donaldson helped Officer Smith to carefully put Perry down on the living room floor. Officer Jones, close behind him, placed Madeline just a few feet away.

"What should we do? What can I do to help?" Mrs. Donaldson asked. "What's wrong with them?"

"We're not sure yet, but the ambulance is on the way," Officer Smith replied. "It should be here any second."

DISPATCHER: "Update for first aid call; location changed to 610 Chambers Road."

Our first aid crew, including Alec Waters, Dillon Chapman, Colleen Harper, and myself, pulled up in front of a sturdy red brick home just a few blocks away from the grammar school. I recalled that when I was younger, I used to pass the house on my bicycle on the way to school each day.

"This is the Donaldsons' house," Alec said, grabbing an oxygen tank.

"I thought so," Dillon replied, lifting the suction equipment from its shelf. "I think one of their kids was a year ahead of me in school."

"Let's see what we've got," Colleen said, leading the way. "Alec and Andrea, you take one patient, and Dillon and I will take the other."

The Donaldsons' front door was wide open. I leapt up two front porch steps and entered their home, lugging the heavy first aid kit with me. I wasn't sure what to expect and said a quick silent prayer that our patients would be okay.

"Your patients are the Parkers from next door," Officer Smith said. "Mrs. Parker is unconscious and her husband is close to it."

I recognized Mrs. Parker right away. She was one of my mom's summertime "pool friends." *Her lips are cherry red, and definitely not from lipstick. Is this a case of carbon monoxide poisoning?*

Carbon monoxide is a very dangerous colorless, odorless gas. Carbon monoxide poisoning is the most common type of poisoning in the United States. Symptoms can include headache, dizziness, nausea and vomiting, weakness, chest pain, and confusion. If a patient has carbon monoxide poisoning, his red blood cells replace oxygen with carbon monoxide. This blocks oxygen from entering the body, leading to loss of consciousness and death. Cherry red lips are a classic sign of carbon monoxide poisoning.

Alec knelt down next to Mrs. Parker and opened her airway. "She's got a pulse, but she's not breathing," he said, and he began to deliver mouth-to-mouth rescue breathing. "Grab the ambu bag."

I quickly assembled the ambu bag, which is a face mask with an attached bag and an oxygen reservoir. It provides a protective barrier between the patient and rescuer and also allows 100 percent oxygen to be delivered, instead of the 16 percent that you can deliver with mouth-to-mouth rescue breathing. I placed it over Mrs. Parker's face and held the mask in place while Alec began squeezing the bag and giving her rescue breaths. *Please, please, Lord, let my mom's friends live.*

I glanced over at Mr. Parker. He lay on his side just a few feet away. While Dillon prepared to place Mr. Parker on oxygen, Colleen checked his pulse and blood pressure.

"My chest hurts," I heard him say softly. With that, tremendous shudders wracked his body and he began vomiting. Colleen held an emesis basin in front of him with one hand and gently stroked his head with her other.

I turned my attention back to Mrs. Parker. "Wake up," I urged, stroking her hand. I tried to squelch the fear inside me that my mom's friend was going to die. Panicking would not bring her back. I knew I needed to stay calm and focused.

Alec provided several more rescue breaths. "I think she may be trying to take a breath on her own," he said. "Come on Madeline, hang in there. Andrea, why don't you grab a set of vital signs?"

"Blood pressure 140 over 86, heart rate 100, strong and regular," I said. *That's a pretty good pressure. Maybe Mrs. Parker has a chance...*

Over the next several minutes, Madeline's breathing became stronger and more regular. Alec switched her over to oxygen via a nonrebreather mask. From looking at her husband, I knew what to expect next. So when Madeline began vomiting, I had an emesis basin all ready for her.

"We need to package her up and get going," Alec said. Officer Smith and Alec lifted Madeline up and placed her on our stretcher. At that precise moment, Madeline Parker opened her eyes.

"What happened?" she whispered. She appeared weak and frightened. "Where's Perry?"

"He's okay," Alec assured her, pointing toward her husband. Perry was already strapped into our other stretcher. "You're both going to be fine," he reassured her.

I know she's not out of the woods yet, but thank You, God, for giving her a second chance! The next hour would prove critical for her full recovery.

"We're not exactly sure what happened tonight, but we think you may have had too much carbon monoxide. We're going to take you to the hospital right now," Alec explained. Turning to me, he suggested, "Why don't you ride up to the hospital with Mr. Parker while we finish up here with his wife?"

"Sounds good," I answered. I was glad to have the opportunity to ride along. I really wanted to see how each of them made out at the hospital.

Dillon and Officer Jones lifted Mr. Parker into the back of one of our ambulances. I climbed in and switched him over to our on-board oxygen. After I adjusted his pillow, I sat down on the ambulance bench beside him and took another set of vital signs.

"I just don't understand," he said as we began our trip to Bakersville Hospital. "We got back from food shopping. A little while later, Madeline said she had a headache and didn't feel well. I wanted to get up to help her, but then I realized I couldn't stand up myself. Thank God the phone was right next to me. I got scared and called the police, but it was so hard to speak…" Mr. Parker's voice shook with emotion. I couldn't begin to imagine the ordeal he was going through tonight.

"Thank goodness you're okay now," I said, squeezing his hand. "Your wife is doing much better too. We think you may have carbon monoxide poisoning, but the police are investigating."

"Carbon monoxide?" he asked with surprise. "How?"

Before I could answer him, my pager went off. We had another call at Mr. Parker's residence:

> **DISPATCHER:** "Request for the fire department and first aid at 608 Chambers Road for a car left on in the garage. Possible carbon monoxide."

"It sounds like you may have accidentally left your car running in the garage," I said. I surmised that they forgot to turn off their car when they returned home from food shopping. The carbon monoxide then built up to a dangerous level.

I left my pager frequency open so that I could hear what was going on back at Mr. Parker's home. "Sounds like the fire department just gained access to your garage," I told him.

"I can't believe we left our car running," he said regretfully, rubbing his chin. "I hope those men don't get hurt."

It struck me then what a kind man Mr. Parker was, placing the safety of the firemen ahead of the well-being of his home. "They have air tanks," I assured him. "They'll be fine."

"Well, that's a relief. Thank you."

"And it sounds like the firemen are also checking your flue to make sure it's not backed up," I added.

"I'm so grateful to all of you."

"Thank goodness you picked up the phone and dialed the police when you did," I said. "You saved your wife's life. And your own life too."

At that moment, the full force of what had just occurred struck me. Had it not been for the quick thinking of our dispatcher, Jerome Franklin, this story may have had a very different outcome. And if it hadn't been for the tremendous courage and heroic actions of Officers Smith and Jones, the Parkers would surely have died that night. Pine Cove is truly fortunate to boast an exemplary police department. These men in blue are some of the finest men I have ever known. They are the first responders to our calls, making sure the scene is safe and initiating care.

I believe that Jesus orchestrated the rescue, ensuring that each of us was available to do our part as we served as His instruments. The Parkers, despite their advanced age, went on to enjoy many more years together!

Manna from Heaven

For it is by grace you have been saved, through faith—
and this is not from yourselves, it is the gift of God.

EPHESIANS 2:8

Luke Moore checked over his to-do list. It looked as though tomorrow would be another busy day. Volunteering at the Manna from Heaven Food Pantry started at 7:45 a.m. After that, he planned to meet his friend Don McAllister for a late breakfast, get a haircut and shave, and then do a little volunteer work at the library. And then he intended to help weed one of the town's garden beds for an hour or so. *Not bad for an eighty-two-year-old. And I love every minute of it!*

Luke, an extremely organized fellow, carefully laid his slacks and polo shirt across the back of his rocking chair so it would be ready for the next morning. Next he folded some laundry and put away a few dishes. After that, he worked on his crossword puzzle for a half hour. He watched a bit of television, read a little, and then decided it was time to go up to bed.

As Luke climbed the stairs to the second floor, a sudden onset of crushing chest pain caught him completely by surprise. Clutching his chest with his left hand, he grabbed the handrail with his right. Cautiously, he climbed the rest of the flight one step at a time. *I need to get to my nitro pills.* The pressure was squeezing his chest so tightly that it grew difficult to get a breath in.

Luke sat on the edge of his bed. Suddenly, he felt so cold and clammy that it was hard to open his nitro bottle. But at last he removed the lid and placed a pill carefully under his tongue. *Relax. You've had chest pain before. You know the routine. Just let the little pill work its magic.*

Luke slowly sipped some water from a glass that happened to be on his night table. Silently, he berated himself. *The doctor told you to change your diet. Said you were taking in way too much salt. Too many hotdogs and too much canned soup. Not nearly enough fruit and vegetables. And now look at yourself!*

The chest pain began easing up a little bit. *Should I take an aspirin? Or should I wait? Should I call 911?* He sat indecisively. He hated the idea of going to the emergency room. It was already late, and he didn't want to be there half the night. And what if he missed helping out at Manna from Heaven? They really counted on him. In fact, he hadn't missed a shift in years.

Luke took an aspirin and then sat back down and waited another five minutes. The chest pain began to grow stronger again. *I guess I'd better call for an ambulance.*

···················

DISPATCHER: "Request for first aid at 12 Shady Grove Lane for a cardiac."

Officer Jack Endicott met us at the front door. Officer Endicott, who was in his mid-twenties, was passionate about his work. He had wanted to be a cop since he was about two years old. He was following the family tradition; his father and grandfather were police officers before him.

"Eighty-two year old male with chest pain. You probably know him—it's Luke Moore. He rates the pain ten out of ten, mid-sternal. It started about ten minutes ago. He's on the second floor, in his bedroom."

I quickly glanced around. The living room looked comfortable, with several beige recliners and a large television. The dining room appeared very tidy, like the kind of room that was only used for holiday meals. Brendan Bentley, Dillon, and I proceeded up a narrow flight of stairs to the second floor.

I recognized our patient right away. I knew Mr. Moore was close to one of my dad's friends, and I was also used to seeing him around town. He was well known for all the volunteer work he did in our community. "Hi, Mr. Moore," I said, patting his shoulder.

"Mr. Moore, tell us what's going on tonight," Brendan said, fishing a blood pressure cuff out of our first aid kit. Brendan was an easy-going guy; I admired the way he rolled with the punches even when things didn't go according to plan.

"The pain hit me like a ton of bricks while I was climbing the stairs. It hurts right here," Luke said, pointing to the center of his chest. "Do you think it might be from something I ate?" he asked hopefully.

"Well, we'll let the ER doctor figure that out," Brendan answered diplomatically.

Mr. Moore looked extremely pale. I ran the back of my hand over his forehead; it felt cool and clammy.

"Is the oxygen helping a bit?" I asked.

"Maybe a little," Mr. Moore replied. "It's hard to tell."

Dillon took Mr. Moore's blood pressure and pulse. "They're both pretty low: 92 over 54 and 61," he said. He printed out a sample of Mr. Moore's heart rhythm from the heart monitor to give to the paramedics.

"I just need to walk over there to my dresser and get my wallet," Luke said, pointing across the room. "Then I'll be ready to go."

"I'm sorry—no walking for you. We don't want your heart to have to work hard right now. Officer Endicott can get it for you," I said firmly. We assisted Mr. Moore onto our stair chair and Dillon and Brendan carried him downstairs.

Dillon hopped into the driver's seat and Brendan and I climbed in the back of the rig. While the medics switched Luke over to their own heart monitor and started an IV line, Brendan filled them in on our patient's condition.

"Nice and easy ride," Brendan called up to Dillon. "We're ready to go when you are."

Mr. Moore settled back in the stretcher and smiled at me. "I feel a little better now. Perhaps I should have stayed home after all."

"I'm glad you feel better, but you definitely made the right decision when you called us," I said. "You need to get checked out."

Mr. Moore grabbed my hand and squeezed it gently. "I know your father. He's a nice gentleman." And then he got a funny look on his face and said, "I'm starting to feel a little faint."

Mr. Moore coded instantly; he lost his pulse and his eyes became glazed. He was clinically dead. *I cannot believe this is happening!*

Looking at the heart monitor, the medic yelled, "V-fib!"

I immediately gave two mouth-to-mouth rescue breaths followed by chest compressions while Brendan assembled the ambu bag. Normally, squad members avoid giving mouth-to-mouth respirations in order to decrease the possibility of germs and infection. However, since I knew Mr. Moore and did not want him to go even one second without oxygen, I acted instinctively. *Please, stay with us, Mr. Moore!*

The medic charged up his paddles and defibrillated at 200 joules. Mr. Moore's body jerked in response. I held my breath. I didn't have to hold it very long. Almost instantly, by the grace of God, Mr. Moore took a few ragged breaths. His eyes opened wide and his arms flew up in the air. "What just happened?" he asked.

"You fainted and your heart briefly stopped beating," Brendan explained. "We re-started it for you."

"Wow—thank you. My chest pain is gone now," Mr. Moore said. "Actually, I feel much better." Color began seeping back into his pale cheeks.

I said a silent prayer of thanks. *Thank You, Jesus.* Mr. Moore was going to be okay.

"I sure am getting sleepy though," Mr. Moore said. "Is that normal?"

"It's normal," Baxter reassured him. "Your body has just been through a lot."

Mr. Moore was oriented to person, place, and time. Since his down time was so brief, there appeared to be no anoxic damage to his brain.

Mr. Moore reached for my hand again and squeezed it tightly all the way to the hospital. "Can you do me a favor?" he asked. "Could you or your father call Don McAllister and let him know everything that happened tonight? I'm supposed to meet him for breakfast tomorrow, but I'm afraid I'm not going to make it." Mr. McAllister was the mutual friend that my father and Mr. Moore shared. "And please ask him to call the food pantry and tell them what happened."

"Of course I will," I answered. "Anything you want. I'm just so relieved that you're feeling better."

In the wee hours of the morning, Mr. Moore was admitted to the cardiac intensive care unit. Five days later, he transferred to the cardiac step-down unit. Two weeks later, he was back to volunteering at the Manna from Heaven Food Pantry!

Some twenty years later I was sitting on a park bench, watching my children play on the swings. I turned and suddenly realized there was a memorial plaque on the bench. I read it slowly: "In honor of Luke Moore, extraordinary community volunteer." My face broke into a joyous smile. And suddenly I felt like Mr. Moore was sitting next to me, enjoying a lovely day at the park.

The Son's Hero

*Surely your goodness and love will follow me all the days
of my life, and I will dwell in the house of the LORD forever.*

PSALM 23:6

Warren Dempsey lounged on the pool deck with his dad. They tossed a football back and forth across the water a bunch of times and then sipped some ice-cold sodas. *This is the life.*

Warren and his father were extremely close. His dad had been his best friend and hero for as long as he could remember. His father had coached his little league and soccer teams, had taught him how to wrestle, and had taken him to tons of football and baseball games. His dad was always there for him.

"I'm going back in to cool off a bit," Philip said to his son. "Care to join me?" Without waiting for an answer, he rolled off the edge of the deck and into the pool.

Warren gazed down into the water at his father. *Why isn't he coming back up? Is he goofing on me?* "Dad, stop messing with me," Warren said. But Philip did not resurface. Instead, he stayed close to the bottom of the pool.

"Dad?" Warren said, his concern growing. "Dad, is something wrong?" Warren slid into the pool and swam down to the bottom. He tapped his father on the shoulder. His dad was looking at him, but was not moving. *What in the world are you doing, Dad?* Warren placed his arms around his father's trunk and pulled him up toward the surface. His father was dead weight. *Why isn't he helping me?*

Simultaneously, their heads cleared the water. Philip gasped for air. "Son, I need an ambulance," he managed to say.

Terrified, Warren yelled as loudly as he could, "Mom, come quick! Dad needs help! Call 911!"

....

It was a perfect summer day. The sapphire blue sky was dotted with cotton ball cumulus clouds and a gentle cooling breeze kissed the treetops. However, the day turned from perfect to grim in a matter of minutes.

DISPATCHER: "Request for first aid at 826 Kensington Avenue for a neck injury."

Gary Meyers, Helen McGuire, Ted O'Malley, and I hopped in the ambulance. "Sounds like we'll need the collar and backboard," Gary said.

"In service," Helen radioed to dispatch. I admired Helen, for she was able to find time to volunteer with the rescue squad despite working long hours as a nurse.

"Your patient is going to be in the pool in the backyard," the dispatcher responded.

The four of us exchanged looks. No words were necessary. We had just had a first aid pool drill a few days earlier. Sometimes it seems like particular drills are jinxed. For example, some years, within a day of our CPR recertification, we have a CPR call. Or we'll train with the collars and backboards only to respond to a motor vehicle accident the next day.

As we pulled up, Ted immediately recognized the house. "It's Sean's uncle's house," he murmured. Ted joined our first aid squad about fifty years ago, and he was familiar with many of the families who lived in town.

"I hope he's okay," I replied. I was pretty sure Sean's uncle's name was Philip Dempsey. Sean belonged to our church, and the four of us knew him pretty well.

We all grabbed equipment and hustled behind the house, where we found a medium-sized pool. Several family members, who looked like they might be the patient's wife and daughter, stood anxiously on the narrow deck area of the pool. I quickly glanced around, but didn't see Sean.

Officer Endicott stood in the water with Philip Dempsey's son, Warren. I recognized Warren from the beach; I thought he may have graduated from high school a couple of years ago. Warren and Officer Endicott were carefully holding stabilization on Philip's head and neck while at the same time keeping him afloat.

I climbed up the small white pool ladder onto the narrow deck and studied our patient. Mr. Dempsey looked like he was about 45 years old. He had short blond hair and a muscular build. He appeared to be in mild respiratory distress.

"I can't feel anything," Philip said. "I can't feel my arms or legs." I could detect a hint of panic in his voice. If I were in his shoes, I knew that I would be panicking as well. From what Philip said, it sounded like he might have a significant spinal cord injury. He was completely paralyzed.

"Did he dive in?" Gary asked Warren. Since Gary was a lifeguard at the beach, he naturally took the lead on the call.

"No, he was lying on the deck and just rolled in," Warren answered. "But then he didn't come up...he stayed on the bottom of the pool. At first I thought Dad was joking around, but then I started to worry. I went in and pulled him up. Then I yelled for help."

I suppressed a shiver. Everyone knows you can injure your neck from diving into shallow water. But I wouldn't have thought you could injure yourself just from rolling in off the deck.

Gary slipped into the pool, careful not to make any waves. He applied a cervical collar to immobilize Philip's neck. As a team, we floated a backboard under Philip and carefully slid him up onto the deck. We placed him on high-flow oxygen and decided to move him out of the blinding sunshine and into the ambulance.

Baxter and Roberta, the paramedics, met us on the driveway and set up in the rig. Gary gave them the rundown on what was going on.

"I'm scared," Philip whispered. I instinctively squeezed his hand to reassure him, but then realized he couldn't feel it.

"We're going to get you to the hospital right away," I said, trying to reassure him. I wished I could promise him everything would be okay, but I knew I couldn't do that.

Baxter started an IV line while Helen gathered a set of vital signs. Philip's symptoms did not improve, but at least they didn't worsen. Roberta assessed Philip's sensation more thoroughly and determined he could not feel anything from the neck down.

We learn in EMT class that "C3-4-5 keeps the diaphragm alive." The diaphragm is a muscle that plays a crucial role in breathing. It's innervated by the phrenic nerve, which arises from the third, fourth, and fifth cervical spinal nerves. Philip continued to complain of difficulty breathing in the ambulance. If he had an injury to his third or fourth cervical vertebrae, we would have had to use the ambu bag to breathe for him. However, Philip was still breathing on his own with supplemental oxygen, so I figured his spinal cord injury was lower than C4, possibly in the area of C5. I hoped it was only a bruise to his spinal cord and that his symptoms were temporary. *Please, Lord, let Philip be able to start moving and feeling again in the ER.* The four of us left Philip in the emergency room with heavy hearts, but with hope.

"Hopefully he didn't fracture anything," Ted said. "Such a nice man, and what a good son he has."

"Maybe they can give him some sort of medication, like steroids or something," Gary said.

"I hope he doesn't need surgery," I added. I knew that emergency spinal surgery was a difficult and dangerous operation.

Our hope was short-lived. Philip's nephew, Sean, called Helen later that day. The ER physician, Dr. Morgan, determined that Philip sustained a fracture of his fifth cervical vertebrae. They immediately rushed him into surgery.

Sometimes, the odds seem stacked against you. During the neck surgery, Philip suffered a ruptured brain aneurysm. Sean said the aneurysm was completely unrelated to the cervical injury. Aneurysms are ticking time bombs which pose a risk of rupturing at any moment. Most people, like Philip, are completely unaware they even have an aneurysm. Unfortunately, Philip's aneurysm burst during the operation. He died instantly.

Sometimes a lifetime of happy memories are consolidated into a shorter time period than we might wish. This was the case for Philip, his son, Warren, and their family.

Patients like Philip Dempsey touch the hearts of EMS providers in a special way. Although Philip died that day, his memory lives on in the hearts of his family, friends, and all the volunteers who answered the first aid call for him.

Charades

It is not the healthy who need a doctor, but the sick.

MATTHEW 9:12

Okay, listen up. Here's the deal," Brendan said. "I just got off the phone with Alexa Cullen from the Harrington Hotel. She asked if we could have a crew ready for a special assignment on Thursday night. Are any of you interested?"

I paused from organizing a container of oral airways long enough to ask, "What kind of special assignment?"

"She really didn't specify. But she was very emphatic that we have to wear our squad uniforms."

"Our dress uniforms or our jumpsuits?" I asked.

"Jumpsuits," Brendan answered with a smile. He knew how much I hated them. I grimaced. Normally when responding to a call, we wear whatever we happen to be wearing at that moment. We have dress uniforms for parades and funerals, as well as squad T-shirts and jackets for everyday wear. At that time, we also had outdated bell-bottom white polyester one-piece jumpsuits. My jumpsuit was a used hand-me-down that was tinted yellow—I assumed the previous owner had washed it once too often in bleach. No matter how much it was washed, it still smelled like old body odor. My older sister had threatened to disown me if I ever wore it in public. "You don't have to worry about that. I wouldn't," I told her. I had already buried it in the back of my closet. Now it seemed like I would have to eat my words if I wanted to go on this call.

Brendan picked three of us to respond to the special assignment: Buddy Stone, Darren Williams, and me. Buddy and Darren had joined the rescue squad about 25 years ago. They were both retired, so they were able to answer many of our daytime calls. Neither of them seemed to share my aversion for the jumpsuits; in fact, they wore them all the time.

"Be at the building at six p.m.," Brendan instructed us. "You need to act extremely professional and do things exactly by the book," he warned. "They want you to seem authentic—like you are really members of the first aid squad."

"We *are* really members of the squad," Darren mumbled. "We shouldn't have to *act* like ones."

On Thursday at six o'clock, Buddy, Darren, and I waited at our building for the "mystery call."

DISPATCHER: *"Request for first aid at the Harrington Hotel for a murder."*

A murder?! I scrambled into the back of the ambulance, eager to get on our way and see what this call was really all about.

"No way is this really a murder," Buddy snorted in disbelief. "They're up to something over there."

Darren nodded his head in agreement. "Pretty strange that they knew in advance that they'd need us right now."

I was intrigued. Of course, as soon as I heard the call go off as "murder," I knew something was fishy. My mind raced with possibilities. Was it some sort of setup? A joke? Or had things really turned ugly there for some reason?

Our crew headed straight over to the hotel. The Harrington was a sprawling, turn-of-the-century gray clapboard hotel close to the beach. Once in a while, my family would go there for dinner. It was starting to hit upon tough times, since visitors to the area preferred hotels that offered more modern conveniences.

"Okay, if they want us to do this by the book, then so be it." Darren, who was driving, chuckled. He picked up the mic. "Dispatch, is the scene safe?"

The dispatcher checked with the police units on the scene. "The scene is secure," she affirmed. "Just go straight to the dining room."

"Make sure you bring in the heart monitor," Buddy called back to me from the front seat. At that time, we were one of the only squads in the area to carry one, and Buddy was very proud of it.

I carried the first aid jump kit and heart monitor, and Darren and Buddy brought the stretcher. A strong ocean breeze pushed us along toward the front door.

Darren pulled the heavy oak door open and we each stepped inside. The main lobby was deserted and the hotel was eerily quiet. *Something doesn't feel right. I don't like it. Where's the hotel clerk? Where is everybody?* "I wonder what's going on?" I asked.

Buddy took the lead. "Let's find out," he said, heading toward the French doors to the dining room.

Buddy swung one of the doors open and we all stepped in. I blinked as my eyes adjusted to the darkness. *Problem number one: Why is this dining room so dark? And where are the cops?*

It didn't take long for me to zero in on problem number two. It was a middle-aged bald man wearing a tuxedo and lying spread-eagle on the hardwood dance floor. Crimson red blood engulfed his white dress shirt and his bowtie was askew. As best as I could gather, the blood seemed to be oozing from a chest wound. We drew closer to take a better look. *Is this really a murder after all?*

Suddenly, a spotlight shone on the three of us. Upon spotting us, the room full of patrons burst into enthusiastic applause and laughter. It only took me a second to figure it out. *I can't believe we're part of a murder mystery theater!* Since Buddy, Darren, and I have lived locally our whole lives, people in the audience recognized us right away. They quickly realized that we were not actors, but rather the "real deal." And they loved it!

"Check pulse," Buddy said, relishing the spotlight.

I knelt down next to our patient and palpated the carotid pulse. It was strong and regular, but I played along with the charade. "No pulse," I responded.

Buddy quickly hooked up the heart monitor. I glanced at the tracing and could see that the victim had a normal heart rhythm. "Flatline," Buddy said. "Should we begin CPR?"

"No way," Darren replied. "He's long gone. Let's get him out of here."

The three of us grabbed onto our "murder victim" and heaved him up onto our stretcher. Amidst another round of clapping and whistles, we began rolling him across the dance floor and toward the lobby.

"Way to go!" a young man hooted from one of the tables at the rear, saluting us.

When we entered the lobby, our patient's eyes "miraculously" popped open.

"Wow, we really are good," Buddy said. "He's alive!"

"What a great save! We didn't even have to do CPR," I joked.

The actor smiled as he climbed off the stretcher. "Much obliged," he said, nodding his head and then disappearing into the shadows.

And so began and ended my first aid acting career. It was the one and only time I have ever worn the hideous jumpsuit in public. To this day, it holds a place of honor in the very back of my closet.

....

"This place stinks of urine," Buddy said every time we entered the local rest home, which was practically every day and sometimes more than once in the same day. And boy, was Buddy telling the truth! Every time we set foot in that place, I felt a pang of remorse for the poor residents. Many of them were confused, but I was sure they still had a sense of smell. Buddy would remark on the odor just loudly enough for the head of the nursing home, a registered nurse named Ramona, to hear him.

Ramona was long on temper but short on skill. One day, her patience reached a breaking point with Buddy. "You're not allowed back in here. You're banned!" she yelled.

It made Buddy's day. "Thank goodness, I've been banned! I don't have to come to this place anymore," he joked. Of course he kept right on answering calls there. After all, someone had to.

I may not have been an EMT for very long, but even I questioned Ramona's skills. Her transfer reports were always lacking in many ways. For example, "The blood pressure is 120 over 80," Ramona would say. We would double-check and it would be vastly different. "Lung sounds are clear," Ramona would report. We would look at her quizzically. We could hear wheezing without even using a stethoscope. "Pulse is regular," she would remark. We would palpate the patient's pulse and note that it was irregular, which we would confirm with our heart monitor. Needless to say, we did not have much confidence in her abilities.

DISPATCHER: "Expedite to the nursing home for CPR in progress."

On the evening of the CPR call, Buddy, Alec, and I responded. *Please God, be with our patient right now.* We rushed in with our ambu bag, suction equipment, and oral airway kit.

"This place stinks of urine," Buddy said automatically as soon as we opened the door.

As we entered the foyer, Ramona was chatting nonchalantly with a female resident. The elderly resident, who was sitting in a chair, smiled pleasantly at us. "Why, hello everyone," she said. "So nice to see some young people around here."

We nodded in response to her greeting. "Where's the patient?" Alec asked. Each minute is precious following a cardiac arrest. We needed to stop chitchatting and get to work.

"This is she," Ramona replied. "This is Edna."

"Excuse me?" Alec questioned, raising one eyebrow.

"This is she," Ramona repeated, brushing a strand of greasy blond hair behind her ear. "This is the patient."

"We were dispatched for CPR in progress," Buddy said, eyeing Ramona suspiciously.

"I resuscitated her," Ramona said proudly. She smiled so broadly that I could see numerous gold crowns sparkling in the back of her mouth.

"You resuscitated her?" I asked incredulously. *There has to be some kind of mistake.* The woman who had been "resuscitated" was relaxing in her chair, happy as a clam, sipping a cup of tea. Edna did not at all look like she had experienced a recent medical emergency, much less a sudden cardiac death.

"I did CPR while she was sitting right here in this chair." Ramona smacked her lips as she warmed to the subject.

"What do you mean?" Alec questioned. "How can you do CPR on someone sitting in a chair?" Anyone who is certified in CPR knows the patient must be lying supine on a hard surface for it to be effective.

"Are you sure she wasn't just taking a nap?" Buddy asked.

Buddy's question ruffled Ramona's feathers. "Of course not," she said indignantly. "And didn't I tell you not to come back here?"

Alec took out the blood pressure cuff and checked the woman's vital signs. Everything was perfectly normal. She was complaint-free.

Ty and Paula, the paramedics, arrived a moment later. In hushed tones, Alec explained the situation to them. I knew from past experience that they were not big fans of Ramona's medical skills either.

"Are you, a registered nurse, seriously telling me that you did CPR on a person who was sleeping in a *chair*?" Ty demanded.

"She wasn't sleeping," Ramona insisted. But by claiming to have done CPR on a person while she was still sitting, she had officially lost all credibility in our book.

We transported Edna to the hospital as a precaution. The trip to Bakersville Hospital was uneventful, probably because there was nothing wrong with her that a little nap couldn't fix.

A few months passed. Alec, Buddy, and I were called to the nursing home for a routine transport.

"This place stinks of urine," Buddy said as we entered.

"Where's Ramona?" I asked, surreptitiously glancing around.

"Oh, you haven't heard?" an aide, whom I hadn't seen before, asked.

All of our ears perked up at once. "No, what?" the three of us asked in unison.

"Ramona's been fired. She faked all her credentials to get the job. She was never really an RN."

She was never really an RN! Upon reflection, I wasn't exactly surprised. According to the aide, she had even falsified her CPR certification. Sadly, Ramona had gotten away with the charade for years. How many elderly residents suffered in her incapable hands? Ramona's dishonesty placed some of God's most vulnerable children in danger. I was relieved to learn that the situation had been remedied.

Please Call a Priest

Even though I walk through the darkest valley,
I will fear no evil, for you are with me;
your rod and your staff, they comfort me.

PSALM 23:4

Sara Brown knew she should call for an ambulance. In fact, she probably should have called for one yesterday. She knew her asthma and emphysema were acting up again because it was getting harder and harder for her to catch her breath. *Maybe I'll just take another puff on my inhaler and see if that does the trick.*

Sara had suffered asthma attacks for many years, but the last time she went to her pulmonologist, he said she had emphysema too. She figured it was from all those years of being exposed to Max's secondhand smoke. *Dear Max, I miss you so much. It's just not the same without you.*

It was no use; Sara couldn't fall asleep. *Maybe if I sit up on the couch for a little while I'll feel better.* She put on her blue fleece robe and slippers and shuffled into the living room. She slowly eased herself down onto her loveseat and then tried to catch her breath. After a few minutes, she still didn't feel any better. *Yes, yes, it's time. I know what I have to do.* Sara picked up her phone and dialed 911.

. . . .

Although I live in a small suburban town, our rescue squad stays busy. We respond to approximately 1000 first aid and fire calls per year. Since we are a shore town, the summer months are the busiest. At any given time, we carry about 20 to 25 members on the roster. Of these, roughly 15 members answer the majority of calls.

Our squad has assigned crews for Monday through Thursday nights to ensure that any emergency calls will get covered. On Friday through Sunday nights, it's all hands on deck. That is, whoever can answer does so. Usually it works out okay. If we can't get out a crew, the dispatcher calls another town for mutual aid.

I was assigned to Monday night crew, but Brendan asked me to cover him that Tuesday. I was really hoping there wouldn't be a call. At the time, I was a senior in high school. It was a school night and I knew if I had to go out, I would be tired during class. I function best on at least eight hours of sleep and final exams were hovering just around the corner. There were only two more weeks until my high school graduation! Unfortunately, even though I was hoping there wouldn't be a first aid call that night, I was awakened a little after eleven.

DISPATCHER: *"Request for first aid at 213 Cherry Blossom Road for an 80-year-old female with an asthma attack."*

Helen hopped into the driver's seat. "I was hoping it would be a quiet night. I worked the night shift last night, and I didn't get much sleep today." She picked up the mic and told the dispatcher that we were "on the ramp."

"Be advised you have one member on location," the dispatcher replied.

I could guess who the member at the scene was. Barry Evans, one of our college-aged members, lived just a few blocks from the call location. It would be easier for him to drive straight there than all the way to our building.

Helen parked our ambulance in front of a small yellow ranch house about three blocks from the beach. As we arrived, our pagers went off again for a different call.

DISPATCHER: "Request for first aid at the railroad station for an intoxicated male."

"Another crew will have to handle that one," Helen said as we stepped inside. Drunken guys vomiting all over themselves are not my favorite type of call. I was glad to be on this call instead.

I glanced around. A frail, elderly woman sat on the edge of a maroon loveseat. Her gray hair was swept back into an elegant French twist. She leaned forward and tugged at the edges of her house robe in an effort to get some more air. I could clearly see the anxiety on her face. *Difficulty breathing must be a terrifying experience...having to fight for each breath.*

Barry quickly filled us in. "Our patient is an eighty-year-old female named Sara Brown. She couldn't fall asleep because of difficulty breathing. Past medical history of asthma and emphysema."

Asthma is a chronic lung disease in which the airways become swollen and inflamed. If a patient with asthma has an attack, the airways produce extra mucous. This makes the airways more swollen and it becomes difficult for the patient to move air in and out of the lungs. Emphysema involves destruction of the air sacs in the lungs. The lungs lose their elasticity and the patient has a lot of difficulty exhaling. We often see both diseases in combination.

Mrs. Brown's blood pressure and pulse were quite high. Even with the oxygen mask, she was struggling to get air. Back then, basic life support units did not carry pulse oximeter units to measure the percent of oxygen in the blood. Regardless, hers must have been well below 90 percent. (Normal is 98 to 100 percent).

"I can't seem to get air," Sara managed to say. Her eyes pleaded with us to do more. Anxiety seemed to emanate from her in giant waves. *Jesus, Sara needs Your loving presence to help calm her fear.*

"The medics aren't available," Helen murmured. "We'd better get moving."

I moved a small end table out of the way to make room for our stretcher. On top was an old photo of a very young Sara with a dashing army soldier. I supposed she must be widowed.

Sara caught me glancing at the photo. "That's my Max," she said simply. For that brief second, her anxiety was replaced with a brief smile of remembrance. I could tell that she must have loved him dearly.

Barry and I transferred Sara from her loveseat to our stretcher. While she was standing, she grabbed Barry's forearm. "I need you to get me a priest right away."

Officer Fred Smith heard Sara's request. Fred had been an officer for as far back as I could remember. He was planning to retire next year and move down south so that he could fish year-round. "Don't you worry, Mrs. Brown. I'll take care of it." He promptly radioed police headquarters and asked them to call the rectory and have Father Roberts meet Sara at the hospital.

Sara's gaze slowly swept across her house. "I'll never see my home again," she said matter-of-factly as we rolled the stretcher toward the front door.

"Please don't say that. We're going to take you to the hospital right now. They'll help you there," I said, patting her shoulder in an attempt to reassure her.

Mrs. Brown nodded, but it almost seemed as if she didn't really hear me. "Please get my rosaries. They're on the dresser," she instructed. "No, wait, never mind. I'll do it myself."

Sara unclasped her seatbelt and climbed back off the cot with amazing speed and agility for someone in acute respiratory distress.

"Sara, no, please sit down," Helen said. "We'll get them for you. You shouldn't be walking around like this."

But it was no use. Sara had made up her mind. I trailed after her into her bedroom, holding her oxygen tank.

"Slow down, Mrs. Brown," Officer Smith chided. "Or we'll have to sign you up for the Olympics."

Sara didn't pay any attention. She lovingly grabbed the rosaries and placed a kiss on the cross. Then she carefully wrapped them around her hands—caring hands that were wrinkled from years of life experiences. She returned to the living room and climbed back onto the stretcher. The anxiety that I had first witnessed was replaced by a look of serene calmness. The rosaries seemed to be soothing her. *The Lord is calming her fears.*

"Father Roberts is on the way, Mrs. Brown," Officer Smith said kindly. "He's going to meet us at the hospital, okay?"

As we crossed the threshold of the front door, Sara closed her eyes. "Deliver me, Lord," she said. She looked peaceful, as if she was going to sleep.

"We've got a problem," Helen said. "Does she have a pulse?"

Sara had a few agonal respirations. These are gasping, ineffective breaths that a person often has as he or she goes into cardiac arrest. They are always a *really* bad sign. Quickly, I felt for a pulse along the side of Sara's neck. "No pulse," I said.

"Begin CPR," Helen said. I scrambled to start chest compressions. *I cannot believe this is happening. I cannot believe she just died. She was just talking to us...*

Barry inserted an oral airway and provided rescue breathing with an ambu bag. Officer Smith placed a CPR board under Sara's head and upper trunk (nowadays, we use backboards instead of CPR boards).

Even as I performed the chest compressions, I could not really believe that I was doing so. Sara had whizzed across the living room floor not two minutes ago! For those few moments, she actually seemed like she was doing much better.

"Are the medics still unavailable?" Helen asked Officer Smith. "We could really use them."

He checked with dispatch. "They're still not available," he confirmed. "The dispatcher will let us know if they become available, but he said that it's doubtful at this point."

Looks like we're on our own this time. We quickly loaded Sara into the rig and Helen began driving us to Bakersville Hospital with lights flashing and sirens wailing.

It's very challenging to perform CPR in the back of a moving ambulance. Helen warned us when turns were coming, but I still felt like I was going to lose my balance. I braced one leg against the side wall and the other against the stretcher in an effort to steady myself. The screws on the stretcher dug painfully into my lower leg. I ignored it.

"Hang in there, Sara," I urged. "We're on the way to the hospital." I knew she probably couldn't hear me, but I figured it wouldn't hurt. After a few minutes, my arms grew tired. "Can we switch?" I asked Barry.

"Sure, let me just recheck her pulse," he replied, placing two fingers over her carotid artery. "I don't believe it—she's got a weak pulse. Hold compressions."

I switched over to the ambu bag and Barry worked on getting a set of vital signs. Although Sara regained her pulse, she remained unconscious and apneic. We entered the ER, and Dr. Morgan and several nurses met us in the code room. We stayed for a few minutes while a respiratory therapist transferred Sara from our ambu bag to a ventilator.

As we were departing from the emergency department, I saw Father Roberts arriving. He was an older priest who cared deeply for his parishioners. He was a living testimony to his faith.

I'm so glad he made it on time. I knew how important it was to Sara to receive the last rites. She wanted everything to be in order should it be her time. We shook hands and I showed him the way to Sara's room.

Dr. Morgan and his team kept working, but made room at Sara's head for Father Roberts to bless her. With loving tenderness, Father Roberts gently placed oil upon Sara's forehead. "Through this holy anointing, may the Lord in His love and mercy help you with the grace of the Holy Spirit. May the Lord who frees you from sin save you and raise you up."

I knew that I was witnessing a profoundly blessed and personal moment in Sara's life. In my heart, I knew that Sara was filled with the spiritual strength and grace of the Lord. *It's in God's hands now.*

I turned away and walked slowly back to our ambulance. Absentmindedly, I grabbed an ambu bag from the supply closet to replace the one we had just used. I knew that we had done all that we could for Sara. At this point, all I could do was pray and hope for the best.

Shortly after we arrived back to our first aid building, Officer Smith stopped by. "I've got some sad news," he said. "A few minutes after you left the emergency room, Sara had a massive heart attack. She didn't make it."

Being a teenager, I wasn't used to witnessing death. I felt shaken up by the call. It's much more common to arrive and find a patient already in cardiac arrest. Once I start speaking to patients, I get to know them and bond with them. Sara seemed like an incredibly sweet lady who bravely faced death with an unwavering faith in God. I tried to take some comfort in the knowledge that she was with her beloved Max and with the Lord. I learned a valuable lesson that day from Sara. I can only pray that I will display the same courage when it is my turn to leave this earth.

Too Late for 911

In you, LORD my God, I put my trust.
PSALM 25:1

Brett Murphy sat cross-legged on the frozen ground and watched as the sun slowly set in the west. A thorny leaf from a nearby holly tree pricked him through his threadbare jeans, and he grunted as he plucked it off his leg. His gaze returned to the sinking sun, its orange glow bidding him goodnight.

Brett shivered, tugging an old wool blanket tighter around his frail shoulders. *I'm really going to miss that sun tonight.* True to the old saying, March was coming in like a lion. The harsh winds mocked his blanket, penetrating him to his very core.

On nights like this, Brett had a bucketload of regrets. *I'm forty-eight years old and look at what I've become. I don't have a nickel to my name and own only the clothes on my back. Why won't I let anyone help me?*

Brett had struggled with bipolar disorder and depression for as long as he could remember. He was supposed to take several medications on a regular basis. When he did, he actually functioned pretty well. The trouble was that he despised taking them. He hated having to rely on pills to function normally. He resented that they didn't mix well with liquor. And most of all, he hated the way the pills made him feel: tired, groggy, and listless.

It was lonely here in the woods. Brett called them "the woods," but it was really more like a large field and a treed lot behind an old out-of-business gas station. Actually, a large highway was only about 100 yards away, and the constant sounds of traffic reminded him of this fact. But here, on this abandoned property, he could be alone with his troubles.

A lone deer stood about twenty feet away, deep in the thicket. He peered at Brett as if to ask, "Isn't it time for you to go home?"

"I am home," Brett muttered to the deer. "This is it, for now. Perhaps, one day, my luck will change." The very same deer often appeared at this time of night. Brett recognized it by its unusual markings on its head and left front leg. He liked to pretend that the deer understood his trouble and that he was looking out for him. It took away some of the unrelenting loneliness.

Brett crawled into a large cardboard box, which he had carefully positioned next to an old spruce tree. He spread a few pieces of newspaper on the bottom of the box to help take some of the sting out of the bitter cold. He hated when the cold seeped through, numbing him to the point where it became difficult to move his fingers and toes.

On warmer nights, Brett lay out in the open and stared up at the stars. Tonight, he curled himself up into a ball and prayed to see the light of day. Unwittingly, his mind drifted to his mother. She was a sweet, kind woman who was really getting on in years. *She deserves so much better than me. She's tried so hard to help. She's taken me in so many times, and I always screw it up. Every time she takes me in, it always ends the same. I lose my temper, the dark rage consumes me, possesses me. I lash out—hitting, kicking, thrashing. She tries to calm me down, but it's no use. Eventually, terrified of me, she calls 911. The police take me away again and I go back to rehab. It never helps. When I get out, the cycle starts all over again.*

Brett turned over onto his side. The box didn't seem to be helping much tonight; it was no match for the piercing March winds. *Mama, I am so sorry. Please forgive me. Tomorrow, I will make it up to you. You'll see; I am going to change. I am going to start taking my medications. I'll go back to rehab, and this time, it's going to work. This time, I'll be open to getting help.*

Almost immediately, Brett felt better. He heard the deer rustling in the bushes nearby and felt comforted by its presence. He closed his eyes and slowly drifted off to sleep.

....

"Andrea, did you hear the news this morning yet?" my mom asked. My mother likes to get up early and read the morning paper, but I don't have time to do that before work. I usually try to catch a brief summary of the news on the radio, but hadn't done so yet on that particular morning.

"No, what's going on?" I asked, buttering an English muffin.

"I just read something really upsetting. A homeless man was found dead yesterday morning in the woods behind the old gas station," she said.

I was shocked. I didn't think there were any homeless people within miles of our home. "That's horrible, Mom. When I drove to work yesterday, I saw a bunch of police cars in the gas station parking lot. I didn't think much of it at the time, but now I wonder if they had just discovered him."

"Quite probable, dear. The gas station has been closed for several years, so I would think that there wouldn't be much going on there. That poor man. It's been so cold lately, especially at night." My mom shivered and buttoned up her sweater.

"I hope he didn't suffer." I felt terrible. I drove by that gas station twice a day and knew there were bushes and trees behind it. I sometimes glanced over and appreciated the glimpse of nature. Never in my wildest dreams did I think some poor soul was making those very woods his home.

"I wonder why he didn't go to a shelter," Mom said. "What a terrible shame. He was only in his forties."

"That's so young," I replied. "I guess he didn't realize how cold it was going to get." At that moment, I realized that homelessness was not just a big-city problem. Homeless people are struggling everywhere, sometimes practically in our own backyard. I often thought of Brett Murphy during the next several months, especially when I drove past the spot where he died.

One morning, I was working at the hospital performing a physical therapy evaluation for an older woman with neck pain. Her face was deeply creased with lines that spoke of either too much sun or too much worrying during her life. But it was her warm eyes that told of her kind, giving nature.

After introducing myself, I led the woman into a private room just off the rehabilitation gym. She took off her black cardigan sweater and carefully draped it across the back of her chair.

"So, Mrs. Murphy, what brings you here today?" I began. Although I knew her prescription was for neck pain, I often start my evaluations with an open-ended question.

"I've been having terrible neck pain for about two months," Mrs. Murphy replied, rubbing the right side of her neck.

"Do you know of anything in particular that may have triggered it, or did it come on gradually?" I asked.

"Well, I've been under a lot of stress," Mrs. Murphy replied. She didn't elaborate, and I didn't pressure her.

I asked Mrs. Murphy about her past medical history and medications. "Well, I have high blood pressure. I take a pill for that, though can't remember the name of it at this moment. It will come to me."

"Do you live by yourself or with family?" I asked, my pen hovering above my evaluation form, ready to jot down the answer.

The room grew very quiet, so quiet that suddenly I could hear the clock ticking on the wall near the door. "I used to live with my son, but he recently passed away," she finally said softly.

I put my pen down. "I am so sorry," I said. "It must be very, very difficult for a parent to outlive a child."

One tear slid down Mrs. Murphy's cheek, quickly followed by another. "You have no idea," she said, and then sighed deeply.

Sensing that Mrs. Murphy wanted to talk more about her loss, I asked, "Was your son sick for long?"

"Brett was sick for a long time, but not in the way you might think. He suffered from mental illness. He had bipolar disorder and suffered from bouts of depression."

I nodded my head but remained silent. Silently I wondered if, in a period of depression, Brett had chosen to take his life.

"My son died of exposure," Mrs. Murphy said, as if reading my thoughts. "You may have read about him in the paper. He died in March, behind the old gas station."

For a moment, I was speechless. This was the mother of the poor homeless man who expired on that bitterly cold night two months ago. *If he had such a kind mother, then why was he homeless?* In my mind, I had pictured the man without any family.

Again, it was as if Mrs. Murphy read my thoughts. "I feel like it's my fault Brett died. I miss him every day, and his death hangs heavily on my conscience. I really did try my best, but it was no use."

"Would you like to tell me about it?" I offered. I knew we were way off track from our physical therapy evaluation, but I also realized that this topic was preying on Mrs. Murphy's mind. I would let her decide herself if she wanted to discuss it more or let it drop.

"Brett was diagnosed with bipolar disorder when he was fifteen, but he was never one to willingly take his medications. When he lived at home, I was able to make sure he took them. But after he turned twenty-one and moved out, he stopped taking them. That's when things got worse for him. He was in and out of mental health institutions almost his entire life. He would do better for a while, but then he would fall back into his old habits…drinking and not taking his medicine. He never could hold down a job for more than a couple months because of it." Her eyes misted over at the memory.

"It must have been very hard for you to see him struggle," I said empathetically.

"He got worse and worse over the years. Eventually, he lost his apartment because he couldn't pay the rent. Of course, I took him in," she said. "It would be okay for a few weeks, or even a few months. But then he would grow so violent that I was terrified of him. In the end, I would have to call the police to help me. Finally I would tell him that he had to go to a rehab or a shelter."

"I'm sorry that the rehab didn't seem to make a lasting change for him," I said. "They're such a huge help for so many people."

"I'm sorry too. And, I believe, so was Brett. But a person has to be willing to commit to make an effort to change. Unfortunately, he couldn't make or keep that commitment," Mrs. Murphy said.

"You tried to lead him down the right path," I said. "It sounds like you did everything you could to help him."

"I took him in many times over the years, but as I told you, in the end, I couldn't let him stay. I was so afraid..."

I rolled my stool closer to Mrs. Murphy and grasped her hand in mine. "You did the best you could."

"But when I think of how cold he must have been that last night, and how he could have been in a warm bed in my home, I don't know how to go on..." The tears fell faster now, splashing down into Mrs. Murphy's lap. "The guilt is tearing me apart."

I reached for a tissue box and silently passed it to her. I had a pretty good idea now of what might be contributing to Mrs. Murphy's neck pain. Figuratively speaking, she was carrying a tremendous amount of stress on her shoulders.

"Have you talked to a professional about how you feel?" I asked. "A counselor may be able to help you through this time."

"Yes, I'm seeing a wonderful counselor, and I think it's starting to help. And I've started going to church regularly. I'm taking it one day at a time."

And that's exactly what Mrs. Murphy did. I saw her several times a week for the next few months. And ever so slowly, as the deep wounds that pierced her heart began to heal, the physical pain in her neck subsided too.

I learned a valuable lesson from Mrs. Murphy and her son. I wonder how many other times we go about our business, completely unaware of other peoples' troubles and struggles. I made a vow to myself to pay more attention to what is going on around me.

Over the next few months, I watched as Mrs. Murphy reconnected with Christ and gradually learned to forgive herself. Although many years have passed, I often think of Brett as I drive by the spot where he left this earth. I pray that his soul is now at rest, and that he has found peace in heaven with the Lord.

Man in the Little Black Box

Answer me when I call to you, my righteous
God. Give me relief from my distress; have
mercy on me and hear my prayer.

PSALM 4:1

stared into my closet and tried to figure out what I was going to wear on my dinner date later that night. I had a little over an hour to get ready, but I still needed to shower and change.

DISPATCHER: "Request for first aid at the Pine Cove Apartments for a 56-year-old man with back pain."

When the call went off, I couldn't help but groan. *I am not going on this call. Someone else will have to answer it. If I go, I'll end up being late for my date.* I pulled a pink and white summer dress off a hanger and pulled out a pair of white sandals. I fervently hoped that I would hear the rig check in service, but the air frequency unfortunately remained silent.

DISPATCHER: "Second request for first aid at the Pine Cove Apartments for a 56-year-old man with back pain."

I stood indecisively in my bedroom. *Where is everybody?* I was really hoping some of our other members would answer, but it was starting to look bleak. I glanced at my watch. *If everything goes smoothly, I can go on the call and still make it back on time to get ready for the date.*

I met one of our veteran members, Buddy, at the building. Since he had recently retired from the banking industry, he answered hundreds of emergency calls each year. "We have to make this fast," he said, tapping his watch. "I've got somewhere to go."

I nodded. "Me too. Fast would be really good."

Buddy pulled the ambulance out onto the apron in front of the building and idled the engine for a few minutes. No one else responded, so Buddy and I rolled. We found our patient in the breezeway between two buildings of the Pine Cove Apartments, flanked by Sergeant Flint and Officer Sims.

Sergeant Flint stepped toward us. "This is Jerry Brinks," he said. "He's fifty-six and lives in Apartment D." Jerry had long brown hair, which was tied in a ponytail with a red rubber band. He had a long brown beard which was nearly as long as his ponytail. Both looked like they could use a good shampoo.

"Hi, Mr. Brinks," Buddy said. "Nice to meet you. Why don't you hop right into our ambulance and we'll get all your information on the way."

Good thinking, Buddy. Let's get rolling toward the hospital, and I can get his vital signs and write up the call sheet on the way. That will save us some time. I wrote down the patient's name at the top of our call sheet, and then looked up to see if he was agreeable with Buddy's suggestion.

"Do you think you're here to see me?" Jerry asked, shaking his head.

"Yes, that's right," I answered. "We were told you had back pain."

"No, I'm not the one with back pain," he said. He sounded like he wanted to add the word *duh*, but managed to hold it back.

"Okay, sir. Why don't you tell us what's going on, then," Buddy said.

"I don't have back pain," he explained. "I called 911 because he does," he said, pointing to a small black box on a rickety wooden table.

"I'm sorry. I beg your pardon," Buddy said. "Who did you say has back pain?"

"He does," Jerry said impatiently, pointing again to the little black box.

"The box has back pain?" I asked, trying hard to keep my facial expression neutral.

"No," Jerry answered. "Of course not. How could a box have back pain?"

Well, that's a relief. I must have misunderstood him. Now maybe we can figure out what's going on and head to the hospital. I glanced at my watch. Fifteen minutes had passed since we left the first aid building. "Okay, so who exactly has back pain?"

"Bennie," Jerry said, as if expecting all of us to know who Bennie was.

"Okay, Jerry. So where is this Bennie?" Buddy asked. "We need to get going to the hospital."

"Bennie is the man inside the box," Jerry clarified.

"Oh," Buddy and I said in unison, both of us momentarily at a loss for any other words.

"What's Bennie's last name?" I asked, my curiosity getting the better of me.

"Just Bennie. He doesn't have a last name that I know of," Jerry said.

Sergeant Flint pulled us aside. "You've probably already figured this out, but Jerry needs to go for a psychiatric evaluation. Hopefully, we can convince him to go peacefully."

Buddy glanced at his watch again. "This call is going nowhere fast," he whispered to me.

"Tell me about it," I whispered back. *Forget about being on time for my date. At the rate I'm going, I'll miss it entirely.*

"Okay, Jerry," Buddy said. "It's time to go. Let's take you to the hospital to get checked out."

"I don't need to go to the hospital. There's nothing wrong with me," Jerry said belligerently. With that, he grabbed the little black box and stormed from the breezeway into his apartment. We followed Jerry inside and found him leaning against a counter in a small galley kitchen that reeked of stale cigarette smoke and burned garlic. The stainless steel sink was piled high with dirty dishes.

When Jerry realized that we had all followed him into the kitchen, he glared at us and stomped into his living room. An enormous black wall unit with a large television dwarfed the small room. Jerry crossed over the worn beige carpet and plopped down hard on a black-and-white checkered sofa. "I don't need to go to the hospital!" he bellowed. "It's Bennie who does!"

Sergeant Flint, Officer Sims, Buddy, and I took turns trying to convince Jerry to go peacefully with us. Unfortunately, Jerry adamantly refused. Time ticked by slowly.

"I have an appointment in a half hour," Buddy whispered to me. "I wish I hadn't come. I'm going to be late."

"Yeah, I'm going to be late too," I said. "But who could have guessed it would take this long?" All of a sudden, I had an idea. "Okay, Jerry, we're going to go ahead and take Bennie to the hospital and have the emergency room doctor take a look at his back pain."

"Good idea," Jerry muttered. "That's why I called you in the first place."

"But you know, if we're going to take Bennie to the hospital, you should really go with him so that he's not alone," I said.

"That's a good point," Buddy said. "We shouldn't leave him here if he's really in pain. And he's going to need a friend to go with him."

Jerry contemplated what we said. After a long hesitation, he said, "Okay, I'll go. I don't want Bennie to be alone. Someone needs to speak for him."

"And maybe the ER doc could take a look at you at the same time," I added.

"Why in the world would he want to check me out?" Jerry frowned, eyeing me suspiciously. "I'm perfectly fine. There's nothing wrong with me."

I quickly backpedaled, afraid I had just ruined our chance of getting Jerry to go to the hospital peacefully. "You're probably right," I placated him. "The doctor will most likely want to focus on Bennie."

While Buddy and I walked Jerry out to the ambulance, Officer Sims walked alongside us, carrying the little black box.

"Please lie down on the stretcher," Buddy directed Jerry.

"Why should I? I'm not the patient. Bennie is."

"But Bennie is in a little box and could easily slide off the stretcher," I pointed out. "He needs you to get on the stretcher and hold him."

"Oh, I get it," Jerry said. "Okay." He sat down on the cot and then stretched out his legs. Buddy and I buckled him in and breathed a collective sigh of relief.

The trip to Bakersville Hospital was uneventful. We placed Jerry into a wheelchair and rolled him to the triage area. Maggie was the RN on duty.

"Hi Maggie," I began. "This is Bennie," I continued, holding up the small black box. "Bennie has back pain." Maggie's eyes narrowed and she drew her lips together in a tight line. She took me by the elbow and pulled me into a small private triage area a few feet away so I could explain the true situation. I told her Jerry needed a bed in the mental health unit.

Well, our way to get Jerry to the hospital may have been unorthodox, but at least now he will get treated. My mind floated to Brett Murphy, whose mental health issues resulted in homelessness and his ultimately death. *At least now Jerry Brinks can get the help he needs.*

Late for School

So Moses cried out to the LORD,
"Please, God, heal her!"

NUMBERS 12:13

Janice, one of my high school classmates, was a sweet girl with beautiful long blond hair and a brilliant smile. She was one of those people who others are drawn to because she radiated energy. Like the rest of us, Janice was counting the days to our graduation.

That all changed in one heart-wrenching second. On a rainy morning in late April, Janice told her mother she was going to make a quick trip to the supermarket. While making a left turn, she collided head-on with a furniture delivery truck. Janice died instantly, and her dreams of the future became buried under a pile of twisted metal and glass. My high school class, a close-knit group, mourned. *Janice's life is supposed to be just beginning. She should have been getting ready for our senior prom and then going off to college with the rest of us. Why did such a wonderful young person have to die?*

A few weeks after Janice's passing, on a beautiful spring morning, I was rushing to get my books together for school. My mom gave me a quick hug. "You'd better hurry up or you're going to miss the bus," she warned.

I hadn't missed the bus yet, but I had come awfully close a couple of times. I ran upstairs to brush my teeth. A tantalizing sea breeze wafted through the bathroom window, hinting that summer would soon be arriving.

DISPATCHER: "Request for first aid at the intersection of Wesley and Second for a motor vehicle accident with multiple injuries and possible entrapment."

I glanced at my watch and tried to do some quick mental calculations. I knew from past experience that if I rode with the ambulance to the hospital, our driver could drop me off at my high school on the way back to Pine Cove. Since there were multiple victims, I knew that we'd need to roll two or three rigs. Sometimes it's tough to get enough members in the early morning, and I figured we would need a bunch for this call. Ultimately, I made a split-second decision to risk being late for school. I grabbed my book bag and rushed out the door.

"I hope they're all okay," my mom called after me. "I can drive you to school if necessary."

We rolled all three ambulances to the accident. As we pulled up, I was shocked at the scene before me. I had responded to quite a few fender benders, but this was the first serious accident. I said a quick silent prayer that everyone would be okay. I could see that a blue van and a small red sports car were entangled in the intersection. The front of the sports car looked like a crumpled accordion. The van, which had come to rest next to a telephone pole, also had extensive front-end damage. Briefly, I wondered if the sports car had blown a stop sign. At this point, it was difficult to tell.

Two high school students, a brother and his younger sister, sat huddled together in the front of the van. Although I live in a small town, they didn't look familiar to me. The boy, who was the driver, looked plain scared. I saw a bit of blood trickling from a cut on his forehead. His sister, who was crying softly, clutched her left arm close to her chest. *Thank goodness, at least they look like they're going to be all right.*

Meg Potter was the first aid officer in charge of the scene. Although Meg was softspoken, she really knew how to effectively run an emergency call. Pointing to four squad members, she said, "Go help out those kids in the van." Then she turned to the rest of us. "Alec and

Mason, you're in charge of extrication. And I'll need the rest of you to help out the girls in the sports car," she said.

I peeked through the window of the sports car and shuddered. Two high school girls lay motionless inside, completely unresponsive. One was slumped over the steering wheel and the other lay on the passenger side, crumpled down near the floorboards. Long blonde hair obscured their faces, and suddenly all I could think of was…Janice. *Dear God, please let these girls have a happier outcome than Janice did…*

I angled my head to get a closer look. From what I could see, it didn't appear as though the girls had been wearing seatbelts. A matching pair of spiderweb cracks marked the spots where their heads had impacted the windshield. The steering wheel was obviously bent.

A few members of the volunteer fire department checked for fuel leaks and cut the car battery to eliminate the chance of fire. Mason Chapman, an auto mechanic at the local garage, chocked the tires to prevent the car from rolling. Every second is precious during a serious motor vehicle accident. The clock is running; the patients need to get to the hospital as quickly as possible. Alec tested the door handles on the sports car. "Jammed shut," he said.

Mason briefly tried prying them open with a crowbar, but to no avail. "We're going to need to use the jaws of life," he said. The jaws of life is a hydraulic rescue tool that combines a cutter and a spreader. It is used to first cut a car apart and then pull off the pieces.

I took a few steps back when Mason and Alec started revving up the tool. I wasn't wearing protective goggles like they were, and I didn't want any glass or metal fragments to inadvertently land in my eyes. We drilled once a month or so with the rescue tools, but this was the first time I was seeing them used for an actual accident. *I really hope this works fast!*

A minute or two ticked by, punctuated by metallic grinding noises. Mason and Alec were making good progress. "We're almost there," Mason yelled over the noise of the tool. A bead of sweat trickled slowly down his cheek despite the cool breeze.

The sooner we could start assessing the patients, the better. It was pretty obvious that the girls, who remained motionless, needed urgent medical assistance. The pressure was on. Ideally, trauma victims should arrive at the hospital within an hour of injury. We were now about ten or fifteen minutes into this so-called "Golden Hour."

Suddenly, with a last mighty heave, Alec and Mason wrestled the door off. They'd done their job. Now it was our turn.

"Rapid take down," Meg said urgently. "We need to get them out as quickly as possible."

For regular car accidents, we painstakingly apply a Kendrick Extrication Device (K.E.D.), which is a semi-rigid brace that stabilizes the head, neck, and torso. Applying the K.E.D is quite time consuming. Therefore, in life-threatening emergencies, we skip the K.E.D and go straight for the backboard. Despite my inexperience, I knew without a doubt that this call qualified as a life-threatening emergency.

"Names are Mimi and Carla. We're working on tracking down their parents," I overheard Officer McGovern say. Dillon performed a rapid assessment on Mimi, the girl that Meg assigned me to help as well. "She's breathing, but she has a weak pulse," he said.

Mimi looks like she's dead to me. Her eyes rolled unseeingly back in her head and her body was completely limp. I suppressed another shudder. *Janice, Janice, Janice.* It seemed almost surreal to be trying to help kids the same age as me. *I should be on my way to school, shouldn't I?* Eight short months ago, I wouldn't have had the foggiest idea what to do. Now, because of a chance conversation with another first aid member who convinced me to join the rescue squad, the Lord had led me down a different path. And so here I was, ready to help.

I took a closer look at Mimi and Carla's faces. I definitely didn't know them. I figured they must be juniors or seniors at a high school other than mine.

While one team worked on Carla, Meg, Dillon, and I focused our efforts on Mimi. I held stabilization on Mimi's head and neck while Meg applied a cervical collar. If I didn't hold her head up, I knew it would flop down and possibly obstruct her airway or injure her neck. Meanwhile, Dillon gave Mimi high-flow oxygen via a non-rebreather mask. We wasted no time sliding each of the girls out of the car and onto their respective backboards. Next, we moved the backboards onto our first aid stretchers. I grabbed a corner of the cot and we rapidly rolled Mimi toward the closest rig. The cot jerked a bit when one wheel struck a rough patch on the road, but I managed to hold on to my corner and steady it.

"One, two, three," Mason said, and then he and Dillon hoisted the stretcher into the ambulance. Meg was already inside, turning on the onboard oxygen. I climbed in next to her and handed her the oxygen tubing from the portable tank.

"Uh-oh," Meg said. "We're going to need the ambu bag." I quickly glanced at Mimi. No more rise and fall of her chest. *She's not breathing anymore!*

I brushed blood-smeared hair away from Mimi's face. I was horrified. I definitely did not want this girl, or anyone, for that matter, to die in front of me. Not if I could help it. My mind drifted yet again to Janice, and I hoped that this would not be a replay of my classmate's accident. *Dear Lord, please let this girl live...*

Carefully, Meg performed a modified jaw thrust to open Mimi's airway. In contrast to the regular head-tilt, chin-lift maneuver, the modified jaw thrust protects the cervical spine in case of spinal injury. Using the mask of the ambu bag, Meg created a seal over Mimi's mouth and nose while at the same time maintaining an airway. "Andrea, you can start squeezing the bag," she said to me.

So while Meg held the face mask, I initiated rescue breathing, squeezing the ambu bag firmly once every five seconds. It was one of the first times I had ever performed rescue breathing, so I took great care to make sure I performed the technique correctly. The seconds seemed to tick by slowly. I wondered if Officer McGovern had gotten hold of Mimi's parents yet. Were they on the way here? Were they going to meet us at the hospital? *If I were one of Mimi's parents, I would be scared half to death right now.*

Just then, the paramedic crew arrived from Bakersville Hospital. I was glad to see it was Ty and Paula. Paula hopped into our ambulance while Ty rushed over to help Carla in our other rig. "Tell me what you've got," Paula said as she grabbed equipment out of her blue airway kit.

Meg quickly brought her up to speed. "Blood pressure 90 over 60," she finished.

Paula palpated Mimi's pulse near her left wrist. "I've got a decent radial," she said. "Keep bagging her."

Long minutes slowly dragged by. The ticking of the clock on our ambulance wall seemed unusually loud. I focused on squeezing the ambu bag and praying for a medical miracle. *I know You're with us right now, Jesus.*

"It looks like she's trying to take a breath," Meg said. "That's a good sign."

No sooner were the words out of Meg's mouth than Mimi's eyes suddenly popped open. Confused, she glanced wildly around the ambulance. Within a flash, she went from unresponsive to wildly thrashing her arms and legs. She strained hard against the backboard straps, hysterically trying to free herself. "No! No! No!" she screamed over and over.

I knew from my first aid class that when a person has a head injury, she may become combative. Mimi now gave us a front-row seat to this phenomenon. She was giving our backboard straps a run for their money.

"It's okay, honey. You've been in a car accident," Paula tried to explain soothingly. She worked hard to keep the IV line that she had just placed from getting accidentally ripped out.

Mimi did not comprehend Paula's words, but we nevertheless tried our best to calm her fears. It was disconcerting to see her staring vacantly and screaming the word "No!" over and over again. However, I was so relieved that Mimi was actually breathing on her own that her yelling was a welcome change.

Mimi's right hand shot out and grabbed hold of my forearm, squeezing so hard that I knew it would leave a mark. I carefully pried her fingers off one by one. "Let go, Mimi," I said. I knew she didn't understand me and wasn't really aware of what she was doing, but I figured the request was worth a try.

We switched the ambu bag back to high-flow oxygen via a nonrebreather mask. Mimi kept trying to pull it off her face, but we managed for the most part to keep it on her. Meg and I took turns patting Mimi's shoulder and speaking soothing words to her, which seemed to help a little bit. She turned to me and seemed to really see me (and not vacantly through me) for a brief moment. "Where's my mom?" she asked.

"She's going to meet us at the hospital," I answered. "We'll be there in just a couple of minutes."

"Everything is going to be okay," Meg added, gently squeezing Mimi's hand.

I breathed a sigh of relief. Meg was right. *Everything's going to be okay. Mimi's going to make it.* It appeared as though our prayers for Mimi were being answered. On that special morning, I received the gift of witnessing the Lord's healing presence as He cared for one of His children.

Our ambulance pulled into a parking space in front of the ER. As we pulled Mimi's stretcher out of our ambulance, some of our other squad members were pulling Carla out from our other rig. I was relieved to see that she was also now awake and moving her arms and legs. We delivered the girls to the emergency room staff without further incident. *Thank You, God.*

"We'd better get you to school," Alec said. "I don't want to be considered a bad influence on you, first getting you to join the squad and then making you late for school." He laughed.

School. The word brought me from my post-call high back to earth with a thud. I glanced at my wristwatch. The call had taken a really long time. My elation at being part of such a great save was now dampened by the fact that I was most definitely late for school.

I trudged to the main office to get a late slip prior to going to class. Straightening out my uniform as best as I could, I checked to make sure it didn't have any obvious blood stains. Bracing myself, I entered the main office. *At least I have a decent excuse. And anyway, it was totally worth it.* If given a choice, I would do it all over again, regardless of being late.

"You're late. What's the reason?" our school secretary, Mrs. Tanner, asked as she began filling out the top of the late slip. Mrs. Tanner was a kind but no-nonsense staff member. She pushed her metal-framed glasses up from the tip of her nose and looked at me expectantly.

I squirmed uncomfortably. I had to say something but also had to maintain patient confidentiality. I decided not to go into too much detail, even though it was probably going to be in tomorrow's paper anyway. "There was this really bad accident," I began.

The busy hum of the office turned suddenly quiet as the rest of the faculty members turned to look at me. I gave them a brief account of what had transpired that morning.

Mrs. Tanner smiled. "Wow. Forget the late slip. Just get to class."

We learned a few weeks later that all four students made a full recovery. I couldn't help Janice, but I was glad I was there to help Mimi and Carla. *Rest in peace, dear Janice. We will never forget you.*

A Day in the Life of a Mobster

My eyes grow weak with sorrow; they fail because
of all my foes. Away from me, all you who do evil, for
the LORD has heard my weeping. The LORD has heard
my cry for mercy; the LORD accepts my prayer.

PSALM 6:7-9

Johnny leaned back in his chair by the hotel poolside and sighed. When had life become so complicated? Ever since he turned thirty, it seemed like it was one thing after another. And then there was that accident, which screwed up his leg, and now he had to walk with a cane like an old man. He felt at times like the pressure was strangling him, pushing him to his very limit. His father spent his whole life building up the family business, and now Johnny felt like he was struggling to try to keep it together. He was happy to have these few days to hang out here with his little sister, Minnie, and just get away from it all.

Johnny glanced at his watch. It was very late…time to go up to bed. *It's a really warm night…maybe I'll take a quick dip before I go up.* He was glad he had on a pair of swimming trunks underneath his shorts. He pulled off his shirt and shorts and hung them carefully over the back of his chair, next to his cane. He removed his wallet from his pocket and placed it on the table, next to his glasses.

Ahhhh…now this is more like it. Johnny closed his eyes and leisurely floated in the pool. His troubles seemed to slowly melt away.

What was that noise? Startled, Johnny peered out into the darkness. "Is anyone there?"

There was no response. Without his glasses, Johnny couldn't see much of anything. Shrugging, he closed his eyes once more and relaxed.

....

DISPATCHER: "First aid requested for a man on the bottom of the Pine Cove Hotel pool."

I couldn't believe my ears. Surely I heard the transmission incorrectly. *Man on the bottom of the pool?! How? Why?* I popped in my contact lenses and got dressed as quickly as possible.

By the time I was in my car, my pager went off again. I anticipated that the dispatcher was going to say, "Expedite—CPR in progress." Instead, he merely repeated the nature and location of the call.

I hope this is all some kind of mistake. Maybe some guy was fooling around and someone saw him and thought he was drowning, but then he swam back up to the surface.

Gary, Helen, Buddy, and I squeezed into the ambulance, along with Barry, Dillon, Darren, Ted, and Jose. Jose, new to the area, had joined the squad a few months ago.

"I wonder what's going on," Helen said. "Do you think he's still on the bottom of the pool?"

"I hope by now someone's gotten him out," Barry said.

"Or he already got himself out," Dillon suggested.

"Well, we'll find out in about thirty seconds," Buddy said as we pulled up to the side entrance of the hotel.

As we trekked over to the outdoor pool, I was hoping to see our patient chatting with our police officers. Instead, I saw a police officer from a neighboring town standing in the shallow end of the pool while Sergeant Derrick Flint stood close by on the pool deck.

Our patient was on the very bottom of the pool in the deep end, directly over the drain. "He was last seen at three o'clock," Sergeant

Flint said, glancing briefly at his wristwatch. "Now it's five. Someone said he'd been drinking all night. We figure he's long gone."

Gary and I looked at each other. We were both certified as life-guards. "You or me?" he asked.

"It might be better if it's you. I'm wearing contacts and I'm afraid they'll come out if I open my eyes under water," I answered. "But I will if you don't want to." I figured Gary would be better at it anyway. I was certified, but I had never actually worked as a lifeguard the way he did.

"It's okay," he said, peeling off his shirt. "I've got it."

"I'll jump in if you need me to," I added.

Gary's head disappeared below the surface of the pool. We all crowded along the pool's edge to watch. It was hard to see, but less than a minute later, Gary emerged. He was towing a dark-haired man under his arm. Gary swam to us, and we all pulled the patient up onto the concrete deck.

I was shocked to see how young the man looked. He couldn't have been more than thirty-five. He was very tan, but the pallor of death clung to him. We all knelt down around him.

"No pulse," Helen said, feeling his carotid artery. I couldn't say I was surprised by her announcement.

"Begin CPR," she said. If we know a patient has definitely been "down" a long time and he shows obvious signs of death, like rigor mortis and lividity, we won't initiate CPR. This man was a little bit stiff already. However, all bets are off for people who die in water. There is an old first aid saying about people who are pulled from water: "The patient is not dead until he is warm and dead." This man's skin was cool. He was also very young. We decided to work him.

I noticed the man's chest was very hairy. The medics would have to shave him if they planned to defibrillate or put a heart monitor on him. Water dripped off his torso and formed puddles on the ground. Jose grabbed a towel and began drying him off; water and electricity from the defibrillator would not mix!

I slid in an oral airway and Helen began rescue breathing while Gary performed chest compressions. So far, it didn't look promising.

"His name is Johnny," Sergeant Flint said. "I'm going into the hotel to get his sister."

Paramedics Ty and Paula arrived in short order. "Let's get him intubated," Paula said.

Ty applied the heart monitor. "Asystole—no shock indicated," he said. Asystole means "flat-line;" that is, no electrical activity is present in the heart.

We took turns performing CPR. After performing chest compressions for a few minutes, I stood back to give Ted a turn. I couldn't help but feel any chance this man had for resuscitation was fading away.

Just then, Johnny's sister, Minnie, came rushing out of the hotel. It was obvious that Sergeant Flint had delivered the terrible news. Minnie flung herself upon her brother's chest, crying and moaning in agony. *Jesus, this woman is suffering. Please be with her during this time of sorrow.*

"Please, please, Johnny, wake up. Please wake up, Johnny," Minnie sobbed. "Just wake up for me and I promise everything will be okay."

It was very difficult for me to watch. I hate to see anyone suffer, and for Minnie to lose her brother in such a way was upsetting. Minnie continued to call her brother's name, beseeching him to wake up. I slowly turned away, not wishing to intrude on such a personal scene.

My attention wandered to the table close by. I noticed that Johnny had taken off his shoes and placed them next to a deck chair. He had put his wallet and glasses neatly on the table. His shirt, shorts, and a cane hung over the back of the chair. *That's strange. If Johnny was so drunk, how could he so carefully place all of his belongings at the table?* Also, Johnny was wearing swimming trunks, not regular shorts. That told me he intended to go swimming and didn't just accidentally fall into the pool in a drunken stupor. In fact, it was a warm August night. It wasn't that surprising that he might have wanted to take a dip.

I turned back to Johnny. Sergeant Flint was attempting to calm Minnie down while Ty and Paula continued lifesaving efforts. "Walk with me for a moment," Sergeant Flint said to Minnie. "Let's give them a little space to work." They slowly walked toward the other side of the pool.

I felt uncomfortable, and perhaps some of our other members felt bad too. It was a stressful call. Sometimes in the EMS world, when a sad or stressful situation arises, someone will make a joke in an effort to lighten the situation. I suppose that this was one of those cases.

"It's a mob hit," I heard one of our members whisper. I knew he meant no harm by it; it was simply his way of trying to ease the tension.

The rest of us tittered quietly in response to the joke. "I cannot believe you just said that," Helen whispered back.

Even though we were still working on Johnny, I knew without a doubt that he was a goner with a capital G. I wondered whether he was married and whether he had any young children. Once again, I said a quick silent prayer for his family.

We tried in vain for another 15 minutes to resuscitate Johnny. Eventually, Paula and Ty pronounced him. We gathered up our stuff and headed out. The sound of Minnie's sobbing followed me.

By the time I got home, it was already time to get up for work. Even if it hadn't been time, there was no way I could have fallen back asleep after a call like that. I took a quick shower and headed over to the police department to work as a beach cop for the day.

The next morning, my mom woke me up when our newspaper was delivered. "You are never going to believe the headline!" she exclaimed excitedly.

She was right. I couldn't believe it. The front-page headline read, "Reputed Mobster Found Dead in Pine Cove Pool." I was shocked. Our member had been joking the day before, but had unwittingly been accurate! Johnny was allegedly related to a major crime family. The death was ruled accidental, but to this day I sometimes wonder.

Seizing in the Rain

*Dear friend, I pray that you may enjoy good
health and that all may go well with you, even
as your soul is getting along well.*

3 JOHN 1:2

Mona Chesterfield glanced at the clock on her dashboard. *Wow—
it's much later than I thought. Bill is going to wonder what on earth
happened to me.* Dinner and drinks had sounded like a great idea when
one of her coworkers suggested it. But now, Mona found that she was
unsure of exactly where she was or how to get home. *I'm starting to wish
I had skipped that last glass of wine.*

Mona made a left turn and studied the scenery. *Did I just pass this
house? Am I going in circles?* She wished there was a gas station close by
where she could stop and ask for directions.

Distracted and confused, Mona didn't see the T-intersection until
it was too late. Her front tires hit the curb hard, causing her hands
to slip off the wheel from the impact. She tried to hit the brakes, but
instead hit the accelerator by accident. *What's happening? Why does it
feel so bumpy?*

Suddenly, the bumpiness was gone, and Mona had the strange sensation that her car had become airborne. The feeling didn't last very
long before she felt her car land with a big splash. *Now I've really done it!*

....

> **DISPATCHER:** "Request for first aid for a car in the north side of Weeping Willow Lake."

The blaring siren of my plectron roused me from a deep sleep. Although I had a pager, I liked to use the plectron (a large emergency response radio receiver) at night because it was much louder. At the time, I was a teenager and sometimes it was really hard to wake up. The deafening blast of the plectron helped me to get up when I needed to. Of course, it usually woke up the rest of my family as well. Then my poor mom would lie awake and worry until I returned safely home.

When I heard the call for a car in the lake, a burst of adrenalin surged through my system and I catapulted out of bed. (Okay, maybe it was more like a fast roll, but you get the idea.) Our squad is fortunate in that we can sleep at home in our own cozy beds at night. Our service area is only about five square miles, so all the volunteers live close enough to respond to our first aid building quickly and get the ambulance to the scene within a few minutes of dispatch.

Car in the lake? Seriously? I blinked at my alarm clock. It was 11:30 p.m. on a Saturday night. My parents, especially my dad, weren't thrilled when I left during the night to answer first aid calls, but they were gradually getting accustomed to the idea. I was a good kid and they trusted me.

I hurried over to the first aid building. Clyde Taylor, a middle-aged salesman who had been on our squad for eight years or so, hopped into the driver's seat. Colleen and I climbed in after him. Mason, Alec, Dillon, Meg, and a few others rolled our other two rigs. We traveled a mile along quiet residential streets and then parked at Weeping Willow Lake, a picturesque, meandering body of water surrounded by elegant homes. I couldn't help but think that Weeping Willow Lake was better suited to ducks and trout than automobiles!

Three fire trucks, with flashing lights and blaring horns, arrived simultaneously with our ambulances. I saw that two police cars were already on the scene. Several of our men in blue stood at the water's edge.

"Mona, stay where you are!" Officer Endicott shouted to the car's occupant. "We're coming out to get you!"

The flashing lights of all the emergency vehicles reflected eerily on the murky water. Floodlights, mounted on our rescue rig as well as on the fire trucks, helped to light up the scene. I could barely make out the outline of two mallards swimming about ten feet away from Mona's car. Startled by all the noise, the ducks began quacking and flapping their wings.

Despite the late hour, several neighbors wandered out of their homes. A small crowd began gathering at the curb to see what the commotion was all about. After all, a car in the lake was not something they got to see every day.

Mona, who appeared to be in her late fifties or early sixties, perched precariously on the roof of her car. The floodlights illuminated her flaming red hair. Her sedan was sinking fast. "Help!" she cried, rocking unsteadily on the top of the car.

"Stay still, Mona," Officer Endicott directed as he waded into the water.

Unfortunately, I didn't think Mona was capable of being steady. Within the blink of an eye, she either jumped or fell (it was hard to tell) off her car's roof into the water. She half-swam and half-stumbled toward shore. Officer Endicott, grabbing hold of Mona's forearm, led her to safety. Dillon and Alec hoisted her from the water onto the bank.

I glanced back at Mona's car. It was now almost completely submerged. Our lake seemed determined to swallow her vehicle as a late-night snack. It was a good thing Mona wasn't knocked unconscious in the accident! If no one had witnessed her accident and if she had been knocked unconscious, she could have easily drowned.

Mona sat on the grassy embankment and caught her breath. Her hair, now dripping wet, hung in clumps in front of her eyes. Her pants were ripped and she was missing a shoe. But luckily, she appeared uninjured except for a few minor scrapes and bruises.

Colleen knelt down next to her. "How are you? Does anything hurt?"

Mona didn't answer Colleen's question directly. Instead, she mumbled, "I somehow missed my turn." The road on which she had been driving ends with a T-intersection at the lake. Rather than turn, Mona accidentally plunged straight ahead into the lake.

"Yes, you missed your turn," Colleen agreed. This time, she reworded her question. "Are you in any pain?"

"I don't think I'm hurt," Mona answered. She shivered despite the warm night air. I placed a small white towel around her shoulders. Dillon began holding Mona's head still in order to protect her neck.

Even though Mona said she was unhurt, we decided to apply a cervical collar and backboard as a precaution, given the mechanism of injury. We weren't clear on whether she had been wearing a seatbelt or not.

"We need the ER to draw her blood," Officer Endicott said. I figured he wanted to find out her blood-alcohol content. "Tell them I'll be there in a little while."

We loaded Mona into our ambulance. "Hop in," Colleen invited me. "We're going to take her to Bakersville Hospital."

"I'll drive," Clyde said. I knew that he preferred driving to riding in the back.

Colleen and I settled Mona into the back of the rig. Colleen grabbed a set of vital signs and I began writing up the call sheet.

"I can't believe I missed that turn." If Mona had been intoxicated before, she was definitely sober now. The alcohol was wearing off and she was both embarrassed and worried. "What am I going to tell my husband?"

I felt a pang of sympathy; it was definitely going to be a long night for her. She would have a lot of explaining to do. I had just gotten my driver's license the year before. If I landed our car in the lake, I couldn't even imagine what my parents would say!

"Well, if it were me, I would tell him the truth and then apologize," I said. I hoped for her sake that her husband was a *really* understanding kind of guy. "The main thing is that you're all right."

Mona lapsed into a troubled silence. After an uneventful

fifteen-minute ride, we dropped her off at Bakersville Hospital's emergency room. I squeezed her hand. "I hope everything turns out okay," I said.

"Thanks," she replied, and then closed her eyes. She looked like she was trying to shut out the whole miserable ordeal.

After we gave the patient report to the triage nurse, Clyde climbed back into the driver's seat and Colleen sat in the front seat next to him. I sat on the first aid kit in between them, in the narrow area just behind the cab.

On the trip home, I heard distant grumbling. A bolt of lightning wove a jagged pattern across the dark sky. I recalled the weatherman had predicted a chance of thunderstorms.

"Looks like we're going to be in for it," Clyde commented as fat drops of rain began to dance merrily across our windshield.

We arrived back in Pine Cove at about a quarter to one. I knew my mom was probably awake, wondering when I would get home. I thought for sure that the call by the lake must be over by now. *Hopefully, I'll be back in my bed within twenty minutes.*

But just then, Mason, the driver of the rig that was still standing by at the lake, called to Clyde. "We need you to come back here. The tow truck is still working on getting the car out of the lake." They wanted us to stand by with them just in case. Mentally, I said goodbye to my hopes of returning to bed soon. *Great. I wish I hadn't rushed out without my raincoat.*

And so, within a few minutes, I joined fellow members Helen and Gary at the water's edge. The light drizzle quickly turned into a heavy downpour. I pushed a strand of dripping wet hair out of my face. My shorts and T-shirt were quickly becoming soaked. As a self-conscious teenager, I knew I was looking far from my best at this point.

"Let's sit in the back of the patrol car," Gary suggested. "I'm getting drenched!"

"Good idea," I replied. "A dry car sounds a lot better than staying out here."

Helen decided to stay by the shoreline, but Gary and I hopped in the back of the police car and chatted for a while. I jumped at an unexpected clap of thunder. "It sounds like it's directly overhead," I commented. I was very glad to be out of the storm. I marveled that Clyde stood directly next to the police car, seemingly unfazed by the storm. He appeared to be deep in thought.

"Andrea, look!" Gary exclaimed. "Something's wrong with Clyde!"

I turned just in time to see Clyde's body hurl backward through the air. *What's happening? Did Clyde just get struck by lightning?*

Gary tried the handle on the rear door of the patrol car on one side and I tried the other, but to no avail. Since we had firmly closed the doors because of the heavy rain, we now found ourselves locked in like prisoners. The barrier separating the front from the rear of the police car prevented us from climbing into the front. We were stuck, unable to help. When we locked ourselves in the back of the patrol unit, we hadn't counted on having to jump out suddenly. Now our brilliant plan to stay dry seemed far from brilliant.

"Let us out!" Gary shouted. We both began banging on the door, but it was hard for the other members to hear us over the thunder and rain.

I watched in horror as Clyde launched into a tonic-clonic seizure. His arms and legs began jerking uncontrollably. His head, which was hanging off the curb at an unnatural angle, jerked spasmodically. To see this happen to a fellow volunteer was horrifying. To be stuck in the back of the car and unable to help made it that much worse. *Dear Lord, please help him!*

Within less than a minute, Alec saw what was happening. He released us from the car and we rushed to help. Clyde's body laid half on the grass and half in the gutter. We struggled to protect his airway and make sure he did not hurt his head from thrashing.

"We need to get him in the rig," Colleen said. A particularly nasty flash of lightning and bang of thunder emphasized her point. Personally, I did not wish to become soggy toast.

When medics Ty and Paula arrived from the hospital to assess Clyde, I climbed out of the ambulance to make room for them. Nervously, I hovered outside with Helen near the back doors of the rig. Paula placed

Clyde on a heart monitor and maintained his airway while Ty tried to start an IV. Though it probably only lasted a few minutes, the seizure seemed to last for an eternity.

Although Clyde was thrashing his arms and legs, Ty was able to start an IV line. Gradually the storm, as well as Clyde's seizure, subsided. He entered a postictal state, which is an altered state of consciousness following a seizure. Postictal states can last for five to thirty minutes or more. Patients may be drowsy, confused, and disoriented during this period. After about ten minutes, Clyde gradually gained awareness of his surroundings. *Thank You, God. Our friend is going to be okay.*

It was Clyde's first seizure. The doctors never could find a cause. However, they theorized that the prolonged exposure to all the emergency lights that night may have instigated it, similar to the idea that video games with flashing lights may cause seizures. It was a scary thought to the rest of us.

I shuddered as a thought occurred to me. Clyde's seizure could just as easily have happened twenty minutes earlier. If this had been the case, Clyde would have still been driving the ambulance home from the hospital and Colleen and I would have been passengers. I had been sitting on a first aid kit without a seatbelt! He probably would have crashed and the outcome could have been very grave for all of us. Life is filled with "what ifs" and "could haves." I thanked God that Clyde and the rest of us were okay. As far as I know, Clyde never had another seizure.

The Loving Send-Off

Have I not commanded you? Be strong and courageous.
Do not be afraid; do not be discouraged, for the
LORD *your God will be with you wherever you go.*

JOSHUA 1:9

What do you think about volunteering on our first aid squad?"
Alec Waters asked me one hot afternoon as we sat in our town's
beach office.

Alec's question caught me by surprise. At the time, I had a summer job selling beach badges. Our beach office was basically an old,
weather-beaten wooden shack alongside the boardwalk. Alec, who
spent his summers working as a beach cop for our police department,
sometimes popped in to visit and take a break from the sun.

"I don't know much about first aid," I replied doubtfully as I swatted
at a pesky fly. To be honest, I had never even given the first aid squad
a thought. I suppose our family was fortunate in that we had never
needed to call 911. The first aid squad was just not on my radar.

"You don't have to know anything about first aid," Alec replied
cheerfully. "We'll train you. And you're already CPR certified." At that
time, almost everyone who worked at the beach was CPR certified. We
took the recertification course together each summer.

"But I don't drive yet," I hedged. My parents were making me wait
until November to take my driving test.

"Don't need to," Alec answered. "Where do you live?"

I murmured my address. Pine Cove is a small coastal town on the

East Coast known for its gorgeous beaches and a quaint town center for shopping.

Alec's face lit up at my answer. "You live two blocks from the first aid building. You can walk or even bike there."

"But I'll be pretty busy once school starts," I said. I was going into my senior year of high school. I was taking a bunch of honors courses and I figured I would probably run on the winter and spring track teams again. I was VP of my school's National Honor Society, a church lector, and a member of the Key Club. I didn't have much free time.

Alec could be quite persistent when he put his mind to something. He had an answer to every objection I raised. "Just put in what time you can. Anything would be appreciated."

Slowly, I felt my resistance crumbling. For each of my arguments against, Alec had a counter-argument in favor of my joining the first aid squad. *It sounds kind of interesting, but I'm just not sure.*

Alec could see me waffling and pressed his advantage. "We're short on members. The town could really use you," he said. "Cadets are first aid squad members under the age of eighteen. I'm in charge of the squad's cadet program, so I'd be the one training you. I think you'd really enjoy it."

Some people join first aid squads because they love medicine, thrive on the excitement, or have a passion for helping others. I ended up joining the first aid squad because I couldn't seem to think of a good enough reason not to.

I've been volunteering for our local first aid squad ever since. I've been privileged to work side by side with some of the finest men and women I've ever known. I've laughed, cried, and prayed with my fellow members. The squad has been an integral part of my life, faith, and family. Joining the first aid squad played a role in my decision to choose a career in the health field as a doctor of physical therapy. Of course, when I first joined the rescue squad, I was too young to realize that it would have a profound effect not only on my relationship with Christ, but that it would also allow me to witness some truly extraordinary "God-moments" in the lives of others.

....

Rosalyn Richards woke up feeling especially tired. She glanced at the alarm clock on her antique maple end table. Half past eight. *Time to get up for church.*

She sat on the edge of the bed, willing her legs to cooperate with her attempt at getting up. "What on earth is wrong with me today?" she wondered aloud. "Hopefully nothing that a hot cup of tea can't fix."

Rosalyn dragged herself to the kitchen and plopped down into a chair to rest. After a few minutes, she stood up, buttered a roll, and made a cup of green decaf tea. But when she sat down to eat, she found she had no appetite.

She shrugged. "Guess I better get ready for church," she said to her small tabby cat, Whiskers. Rosalyn had gotten into the habit of talking to Whiskers ever since her husband passed away four years ago.

As Rosalyn shuffled back to her bedroom, she paused to study a large framed photograph on the wall. It was a picture of her latest family reunion, a wonderful gathering that took place each summer. Looking at the photo of her four children, their spouses, and all of her grandchildren never failed to cheer her up. "I just wish they weren't scattered all over the country," she said to Whiskers.

Rosalyn's legs felt like lead and she started to feel a bit lightheaded. *Just ignore it. Keep going.* She pushed ahead, donning her Sunday dress and a pair of black flats.

"I'll be back in an hour, Whiskers," Rosalyn said, clicking the door closed behind her. If she hurried, she would have just enough time to make the ten o'clock service at Good Shepherd Church. *I'll feel much better once I'm there. I don't want to miss it.*

....

DISPATCHER: "Request for first aid at Good Shepherd Church for a woman who fainted."

The message blared out of my plectron, which sat on our kitchen counter. At the time, I was a cadet member of the first aid squad. Cadets are members who are less than eighteen years of age. About 25 years ago, "state of the art" pagers were for probationary and active members. Cadets like me had plectrons, but I didn't mind. The plectron emitted an ear-splitting, high-pitched siren followed by a message whenever there was a first aid or fire call. If I wasn't at home, I still knew when there was a call because the air horn that sat atop our town's water tower would blast an alert. In fact, the siren was so loud that if you lived within a couple blocks radius, you might want to consider investing in a pair of earplugs. The siren wouldn't tell me where the call was, but at least I knew that there was one. I could head over to the first aid building and figure out where to go from there.

"I'll be back in a few…I'm going on a call," I called to my parents, who were enjoying Sunday morning breakfast together. With a shiver, I braced myself against the sharp January wind and ran one long block and one short block to our town's first aid building.

Our building is a two-story brick structure that was donated many years ago by a local family in memory of one of their loved ones. At one time, our building was state-of-the-art. Unfortunately, we were starting to outgrow it. Literally. One of our newer ambulances didn't even fit inside the building, so we had to park it out back.

I thought of the woman who had fainted at church. I've gone to Good Shepherd Church my whole life, so at least I was familiar with the layout. It's a beautiful lakeside church about a mile from our squad's headquarters. I glanced at my watch and realized that the ten o'clock service was already underway. I'd already been on a few fainting calls there. Once, a woman passed out because she got too warm. Another time, a man fainted because he hadn't eaten breakfast and his blood sugar got a little too low. Neither of them ended up going to the hospital.

DISPATCHER: "Update for request for first aid at Good Shepherd Church; female patient with a possible heart attack."

Alec arrived at the building at the same time as me. He hopped into the driver's seat and grabbed the radio mic. "On the ramp," he said.

"Received," the police dispatcher replied. "Be advised you have two members on the scene. Expedite—CPR is now in progress."

Alec flipped on the lights and sirens. "In service," he said as we took off toward the church.

My heart began to thud uncomfortably in my chest and my palms got sweaty. *My first CPR call!* I had practiced cardio-pulmonary resuscitation many times on mannequins, but I knew without a doubt that performing CPR on a real person would be a vastly different experience. I had never even seen a dead person before, except at wakes and funerals. I tried to quell my butterflies.

Alec sensed my jitters. "You'll be fine," he said reassuringly. He parked the ambulance by the side door of the church. We loaded our arms with equipment: the first aid jump kit, an oxygen tank, the clipboard with call sheets, and a suction unit. Alec swung the heavy, wooden door open and I quickly followed him into the church. I blinked as my eyes adjusted from bright sunshine to the dim interior lighting.

I immediately became aware that over two hundred pairs of eyes had turned to stare at us. I bit back a wave of stage fright. I heard Pastor Benson say, "Let us pray," as he began leading the congregation in words of healing for our patient. Pastor Benson had been the pastor of Good Shepherd Church for the past two years. He was well liked for his warm manner and insightful interpretations of the Bible readings.

My gaze turned to our victim. She was an elderly woman lying flat on her back in the third pew. I noticed her face was ashen with a bit of bluish discoloration around her lips. She was wearing just one black flat; I guessed the other must have slipped off her foot when she fainted. There didn't appear to be any family or friends with her.

"Name's Rosalyn Richards," Mason said as he firmly squeezed an ambu bag every five seconds. "She told the woman next to her that she didn't feel good and then passed out. The people around her managed to catch her and let her down gently. When the cops arrived, they started CPR."

Unfortunately, there is not a lot of modesty on CPR calls because the chest needs to be exposed to perform proper compressions. Alec cut Mrs. Richard's pretty floral dress open at the top to allow us better access. Aware that many eyes were upon her, he tried to keep her covered as best as he could.

"Why don't you go back to the rig and grab the backboard?" Alec directed me. A primary responsibility of a cadet is to function as a "gopher" and run back and forth to the ambulance to get equipment. I raced out and grabbed a backboard and straps for our victim. We would need the backboard to transfer Mrs. Richards onto our stretcher. A patient needs to be on a firm surface, like a backboard, in order to receive effective chest compressions during CPR.

As I re-entered the church with the backboard, I was dimly aware that my history teacher, Mr. Lucenza, sat a few rows back. I also spotted a boy, Parker, from my senior class. I felt my cheeks redden with discomfort. I am pretty shy and do not like to be the focus of attention. I crouched down at the end of the pew and waited for someone to tell me what to do next.

"Go ahead and suction her," Mason said to me. For a split second, I thought my own heart was going to stop. *Suction the patient?!* Mason was wonderful about getting us new members actively involved. He said the best way to learn something was to just go ahead and do it. Mason could have suctioned Mrs. Richards himself, but instead he made it a point to give me a chance. Part of me appreciated the gesture, and part of me was terrified. *Jesus, please be with me and make sure I do this right.*

I had practiced suctioning a mannequin with Alec, but I had never tried it on a real person. I could hear Mrs. Richards gurgling and realized I had better start suctioning fast. Sometimes during CPR, air gets into the patient's stomach. This creates gastric distention, which may cause the person to vomit. It is vital to suction the material out of the mouth quickly before it's inhaled into the lungs. Inhaling vomit can lead to other complications, such as aspiration pneumonia.

I glanced down at my hands and hoped they wouldn't start shaking. I attached a suction catheter to the tubing on the suction device and lubricated it by running some sterile water through it. Carefully, I placed the tip of the catheter into Mrs. Richard's mouth. I performed a figure-eight with the catheter for fifteen seconds and watched the fluid drain out of her mouth and down the suction tubing. Slowly, I withdrew the catheter and breathed a sigh of relief that I had done it correctly.

Meanwhile, paramedics Ty and Paula arrived from the hospital. Ty began the process of intubating the patient while Paula set up the defibrillator. Back then, defibrillation was strictly considered an advanced lifesaving skill. Nowadays, these life-saving defibrillators can be found in schools, banks, churches, and other places throughout the community.

"She's in v-fib," Paula said as she read the heart monitor. When the heart is in ventricular fibrillation, the lower chambers of the heart beat very fast in an ineffective, uncoordinated way (picture a pile of quivering worms). Untreated, ventricular fibrillation is a fatal cardiac condition. Sometimes, a person whose heart is in v-fib can be converted back to a normal sinus rhythm with successful defibrillation. Silently, I prayed that this would be one of those cases. *Please, Lord, let this work!*

"Everyone clear," Paula ordered, waving her arm over the woman's body to make sure we were not touching her. I was vaguely aware that the congregation had lapsed into a worried, yet mesmerized, silence. The medic gingerly pressed the shock button. Mrs. Richard's body jerked in response to the jolt of electricity.

"Check pulses," Ty said.

Mason placed his fingers on the side of the woman's neck, checking her carotid artery. "No pulse."

I bit back my disappointment.

"She's still in v-fib. I'm going to give another shock. Everyone clear," Paula directed. Once again, she pressed the shock button and Mrs. Richard's body jerked from the joules of energy coursing through her chest.

"Check pulses," Ty said again.

"I have a weak pulse," Mason answered, palpating the carotid artery once more.

"I've got a weak radial pulse," Alec confirmed, feeling the artery near Mrs. Richard's wrist.

I was so entranced that I briefly forgot we had an audience. It looked as though my first CPR call might actually be a save! *Thank You, Lord.*

Meanwhile, Ty visualized Mrs. Richard's airway and carefully inserted an endotracheal tube. Intubation allows air to directly enter the lungs and avoids further gastric distention. We quickly strapped Mrs. Richards onto the backboard as we continued to administer rescue breathing. As we exited, I could hear the service resume.

We quickly loaded Mrs. Richards into our ambulance. Paula rode with us and Ty followed in their medic truck. Mrs. Richards maintained her pulse during the ambulance ride to the emergency room, but she remained unconscious.

Although Mrs. Richards had been alone at the service, the police were able to figure out who she was from her driver's license. The next day, I called the hospital and found she was in critical condition. A few days later, I kept my fingers crossed and called the hospital again. The operator informed me that they had no one in the hospital by that name. Perhaps it was childish, but I hoped against hope that she got suddenly better and was discharged to a rehab facility. Unfortunately, I read her obituary in the newspaper a few days later.

At the time, I felt really bad that she didn't make it. I felt like that although we had tried our best, it just hadn't made a difference in the end. I made it a point to keep Mrs. Richard's family in my prayers.

A few weeks later, our first aid squad received a letter from Mrs. Richard's family:

Dear Pine Cove First Aid Squad Members:

We would like to thank you for the kind and competent care you provided to our mother, Rosalyn Richards, several weeks ago. We are so grateful that you were able to revive her long enough for all of us to fly in from around the country to say our last goodbyes in person. Being able to hold her hands and tell her how much we love her brought us immeasurable comfort during her final days. It was truly an answer to our prayers.

Sincerely,
The Richards Family

My eyes welled up with tears. The letter gave me a different perspective. I was glad to learn that Mrs. Richards had lived a good, happy life and that she had a large, loving family who was with her during her final hours on earth. *Our actions made a difference after all.* I reflected on how God has a plan for each of us. We were able to serve as instruments of the Lord in that we helped resuscitate Rosalyn long enough for her children to give her a loving send-off.

Thanksgiving

Let the peace of Christ rule in your hearts, since as members
of one body you were called to peace. And be thankful.
COLOSSIANS 3:15

What does Thanksgiving mean to you? In grammar school, I recall drawing cornucopias and writing inside all the things for which I was thankful. Later, Thanksgiving grew to mean time with family, relaxation, and delicious holiday meals. I'll admit, back in high school, I took it all for granted. Now I know better.

DISPATCHER: "Request for first aid at the Pine Cove Apartments for a man with a back injury."

Alec, Mason, and I answered the call. The Pine Cove Apartments, cozy red brick units surrounded by towering oak trees, were at the west end of town. As I stepped out of the ambulance, a crisp autumn breeze chilled the air. Crunchy brown leaves tumbled across the grass and sidewalks of the complex. I picked up a newspaper from the front porch and brought it inside with me.

We found our patient, an elderly gentleman by the name of Mr. Clark, sitting hunched over at his kitchen table. Deep wrinkles, a testament to his long life, lined his face and neck. A newspaper, not yet opened, lay neatly folded nearby. I glanced at the date. It was yesterday's paper. An English muffin and a small glass of orange juice sat untouched next to it.

"Sorry I'm not dressed yet," Mr. Clark apologized, pointing to his blue flannel pajamas. "My back pain is acting up again today. I have an old slipped disc and it gives me trouble from time to time."

It looked as though he lived alone. I hoped he would be getting together with family later. *It must be depressing and lonely to be alone for a major holiday, especially if you aren't feeling well.* "Is there someone we can call for you?" I asked.

A shadow briefly crossed his face. "I'm afraid not. My wife passed and we didn't have any children. I have a few cousins down South, but they're getting old like me."

I began writing up the call sheet while Mason and Alec performed the assessment. Mr. Clark's vital signs were okay: blood pressure, heart rate, and respiratory rate were all relatively normal.

"I feel foolish even calling you all out on a holiday," Mr. Clark said. "Maybe I should just take a few more aspirin. What do you think?"

"You did the right thing to call us," Alec said, patting Mr. Clark on the shoulder. "It's always better to get checked out and be on the safe side. If you felt bad enough to call us, you should probably go to the hospital."

We helped Mr. Clark onto our stretcher and then into the ambulance. Alec had to go to meet his family, so Mason climbed into the driver's seat and I rode in the back with Mr. Clark.

"I've had this back pain on and off for months now," he confided. "But it was so much worse than usual when I woke up this morning. I suppose it's just as well that I'm getting help for it."

As we pulled up to the emergency room, I asked, "How's the pain doing now?"

"I think it's easing up a bit," he replied.

"Well, I'm glad to hear that and I'm also glad that you're getting checked out," I said. "Do you have any friends or neighbors who can check in on you when you get home?"

Mr. Clark frowned. "No, I've been keeping pretty much to myself lately. Seems like my friends have been passing on, one by one. That's the trouble when you get old like me."

I felt really bad for Mr. Clark. Here I was, about to go home to a delicious traditional Thanksgiving meal. It sounded to me like Mr. Clark would be going home to a can of soup and some crackers. Alone. *How many other people are alone on this holiday? How many of them go to the emergency department to avoid being alone?*

"Thank you very much for all your help," Mr. Clark said, patting my hand as we rolled the stretcher down the long hallway to the emergency room. "I'm sorry I took you away from your family."

Mason gave the report to the triage nurse while I said goodbye to Mr. Clark. "Hopefully you'll be home again and feeling better in a few hours."

"Please say a prayer that I do," he said, grimacing. "I hate hospitals."

I gave his hand a quick squeeze. "I promise I will," I said. "You'll be at the top of my list."

An hour later, we responded to a first aid call for a gentleman who fell and scraped his head. I looked around when we got to the emergency room, but I didn't see Mr. Clark. *I guess he must be in a cubicle somewhere. I'm glad he's getting treated.*

I was home a little after one. The delicious aroma of turkey wafted into my nostrils the moment I opened the door. I thought of Mr. Clark, and felt a little stab of guilt. *I have so much to be thankful for.* Later on in the evening, after a wonderful Thanksgiving meal with my family, I was surprised when we were dispatched to return to Mr. Clark's apartment.

DISPATCHER: "Request for first aid at the Pine Cove Apartments for an elderly man with stomach pain."

This time, Mason and I found Mr. Clark doubled over on a blue plaid sofa in his living room. I was sad, but not surprised, to see that he was alone. A glass of water, seemingly untouched, stood close by on his end table. His skin was a sickly shade of pasty white and he felt cold and clammy to the touch. I felt the first stirrings of unease.

"Mr. Clark, what's happened since we last saw you?" I asked. "I was hoping that you would be feeling much better by now."

"The ER sent me home with some pain pills, but my back pain is getting worse and worse," he explained. "It feels like my back is on fire. Now, my stomach hurts too and I noticed that it's starting to bulge out." He gently rubbed his stomach as he spoke.

Mason pulled up Mr. Clark's shirt and we took a look. Right away, I could see that he had a large pulsating mass just above his belly button. *What in the world is that?* I had never seen anything like it. But I knew beyond a doubt that it couldn't be a good thing. I wondered if it had been there this morning when we transported him. If so, he hadn't mentioned it and we hadn't noticed it.

While Mason placed Mr. Clark on high-flow oxygen, I knelt down next to him to check his vital signs. His blood pressure was low and his pulse was weak and rapid. I couldn't help but think he seemed a lot worse than the first time we brought him in. *What is going on with him?*

Once again, we assisted Mr. Clark onto our stretcher. This time, his legs were much shakier. In the back of the rig, I held Mr. Clark's hand. It was the best way I could think of to comfort him. He seemed frightened, and I was frightened for him.

"My wife, Lula, passed away ten years ago this month," he said. "I feel so alone."

I felt a lump form in my throat and I couldn't seem to get any words out. Instead, I squeezed Mr. Clark's hand harder.

"It wouldn't be the worst thing if it was my time to meet her, you know. I've had a really good life. The Lord has been good to me and for that, I'm thankful."

I kept Mr. Clark on high-flow oxygen and kept checking his blood pressure and pulse. His blood pressure was tanking, but his pulse kept climbing higher. I breathed a sigh of relief when we pulled into the emergency room parking lot. Within a moment, Mason and I were rolling down the hallway into the ER. Again.

"He's got stomach pain and this really large, pulsating mass," Mason said to the triage nurse, Maggie.

Maggie, a veteran nurse with a keen eye for detail, abruptly stood up from her chair behind the triage desk and pulled up Mr. Clark's shirt to take a closer look herself.

"I need Dr. Morgan stat," she barked. Her fingers slid to Mr. Clark's wrist and she felt for his radial pulse.

I was glad Dr. Morgan was on duty. *Dr. Morgan is one of the best. If anyone can help Mr. Clark, he can…*

Mason and I quickly rolled Mr. Clark into one of the triage rooms. A different crew was working than the first time we brought Mr. Clark in. I switched the oxygen from our portable unit to the hospital's supply as Dr. Morgan performed his assessment. *I don't want to leave Mr. Clark. He seems so alone.* I felt unsettled as I stepped out of the triage room. Unwilling to leave just yet, I hovered in the hallway. A few moments later, Dr. Morgan and Maggie also stepped out of the room.

"It's a massive AAA, and it looks like it may have ruptured," I heard Dr. Morgan say. Later, I found out that stands for *abdominal aortic aneurysm.* "I doubt it's operable," he added. "He's probably only got a few hours to live, maybe less. Maggie, I need you to get the thoracic surgeon on call to take a look at him right away."

I was horrified. What do you do if you only have a few hours to live? I took one more peek in past the curtain. Two emergency room nurses were making Mr. Clark as comfortable as possible. *I know that he's in good hands and at least he won't die alone in his apartment, but I feel absolutely terrible.*

But then, Mr. Clark's words in the back of the ambulance suddenly came back to me. "I've had a really good life. The Lord has been good to me and for that, I'm thankful." I took comfort in the fact that our life on earth is, after all, only the first step in our journey. If Mr. Clark didn't make it through the surgery, then he would be with his beloved wife again. I stepped back into the triage room and gave his hand one last squeeze. Reluctantly, I let go of his dear old hand and turned away. *Lord, please watch over Mr. Clark.*

Thirty minutes later, as I arrived home and turned the knob of our back door, the full force of what I had witnessed struck me. At that moment, I truly understood the meaning of the word Thanksgiving. *I have so much to be thankful for.*

The Bite

*Be on your guard; stand firm in the
faith; be courageous; be strong.*

1 CORINTHIANS 16:13

Janet Schuster roused from her late-night nap on the sofa. *What's that strange noise?* "Sam, is that you?" Janet Schuster called out to her husband of thirty years. Her question was met by an eerie stillness.

Janet and Sam owned Schuster's Second Chance Books, a used-books store in a nearby town. Usually, they worked there together until closing time and then came home a little after six. Tonight, Sam decided to work late on inventory. Since Janet was feeling a bit under the weather, she decided to go home without him. After taking an aspirin and eating a bit of chicken soup, she decided to nap on the couch until Sam got home.

Janet sat up and shivered. She cocked her head to listen, but all was silent. But then, there it was again. A strange, slicing noise...

Janet stood up and looked toward the kitchen. A sense of foreboding filled her and the nape of her neck began to tingle. *God, please protect me.* "Sam? Is that you?" she called out again. "Is someone there?"

Silence filled the air. Step by step, Janet slowly inched toward the kitchen. She flipped on the wall switch, and suddenly the kitchen was illuminated with bright fluorescent light. *That's funny, I don't recall opening the kitchen window.* She shut it firmly and pulled the shade down.

Janet slowly walked back to the living room and shrugged. *I must have imagined that noise.* She sat back down on the sofa, pushed aside a few old magazines, and propped her feet up on the coffee table. Nervously, she twisted her long, gray hair up into a bun. Grabbing the remote, she flipped on the television and decided to wait up for Sam. He was due home in a minute or two.

One or two minutes turned into ten. Janet grew drowsy. And just as she began to close her eyes, a dark figure sprang out of the shadows and lunged at her.

....

DISPATCHER: "Request for first aid at 610 Bartholomew Road for a woman with a finger bite."

I jumped out of bed, pulled on a pair of pants, and slipped on my sneakers. *I guess the lady must have gotten bitten by a cat or dog.* Calls for dog bites were not that uncommon.

Helen McGuire drove and I hopped into the passenger seat next to her. "Hopefully, this is nothing too bad," she remarked. "I was in the middle of watching a movie."

"I was watching a movie about my pillow," I said. "It was really soft…"

Helen made a quick left off a two-lane highway and stopped short. "What in the world is going on?" she asked aloud.

What in the world is right! Police cars were everywhere. I spotted two from our town, two from another, and a fifth from yet another town. Officers were running down the street and through front yards, shining their flashlights. They were obviously looking for someone or something. We live in a really quiet town. Not too much happens here that requires this level of police activity. I felt my adrenalin level surge. I quickly rolled my window down to see if I could hear anything. *This call is going to be more than we bargained for.*

Helen pulled alongside Officer Endicott. "What's up?" she asked.

"We had a suspect in the house and he attacked the homeowner, Mrs. Schuster," he replied.

"Do you want us to go in?" Helen asked. "Is Mrs. Schuster okay? Where's the attacker now?"

"We've just finished searching the house and it's clear. You're okay to go in."

"That's good enough for me," I said. "As long as the attacker's somewhere out here, let's get in there."

Helen pulled up and parked our ambulance in front of the Schuster's home. Their house was fairly small and looked like it could use a fresh coat of paint. A half-dead fern plant lay tipped over on the front porch. The screened door squeaked as I pulled it open.

Helen and I found Mrs. Schuster, a middle-aged woman who looked older than her years, sitting on a faded plaid sofa in the living room. She was visibly agitated, waving her right arm excitedly.

I recognized her right away. I had been to her bookstore numerous times to pick up some light reading for the beach. "Hi Mrs. Schuster," I said. "Officer Endicott told us that someone attacked you…"

"He bit my finger! He bit my finger! He came through that window and bit my finger!" Mrs. Schuster pointed to a window toward the rear of the house. I could see that the screen had either been cut or torn.

"Who bit your finger?" I asked.

"Stephen! Stephen! He came in here and bit my finger!" Her agitation seemed to be growing by the minute.

Goosebumps rose in a wave across my back. I looked behind me and then cautiously peered in every direction. An old lamp provided a bit of light, but it didn't seem like enough. I saw a small closet, an eat-in kitchen, and a narrow hallway leading to a few bedrooms. I wished Officer Endicott was in here with us.

The patient read my mind. "Stephen is gone. I saw him go out the front door."

I breathed a sigh of relief. "Good. Thanks."

Helen and I knelt down beside Janet and took a closer look at her finger. The bleeding had already stopped. Several tooth marks were easily identifiable just below Janet's nail bed. Helen and I carefully cleaned the wound with sterile water and applied a sterile bandage and dressing.

"Why did he bite you?" Helen asked. It was the question I was dying to ask, but hadn't gotten up the nerve to say out loud yet.

"He's my daughter's boyfriend. He doesn't like me. I don't know why. He came in here and bit my finger!" She shook her head vehemently, almost as if in disbelief.

I felt bad for Janet. Domestic disputes are never pleasant. But this one was so creepy…to be attacked in your own home by someone you know…

Helen leaned toward me and whispered Stephen's last name in my ear. I was shocked—I knew Stephen! Although he was several years younger than me, I had seen him around town and at the beach.

"Thank you very much for your time," Mrs. Schuster said. "It hurts, but I don't want to go to the hospital. I'll stay home and wait for Sam. The police officer said he's on his way."

Helen handed Janet our refusal form. Janet signed with her left hand, since Stephen had bitten her right one.

"Make sure you see your physician tomorrow. You may need a teta-nus shot," I said. I was concerned that the bite could become infected.

She nodded, but I could tell her mind was drifting. Perhaps she was thinking about Stephen. I knew I was.

"Are you going to be okay in here on your own?" Helen asked. "Would you like us to stay with you until your husband gets home?"

"No, thank you. I'm fine. Sam will be here any minute. I've already taken up enough of your time." She gently pushed us with her left hand toward the front door. I imagined that she was eager to put an end to this whole unfortunate night.

When we went back outside, the police were still searching for Ste-phen. *Where is he hiding?* I scanned the bushes and trees, imagining that he might jump out at us at any moment.

"Mrs. Schuster doesn't want to go to the hospital," Helen explained to Officer Endicott. "We're taking off. Good luck!" He waved goodbye, and we headed back toward our first aid building. "Can you believe that?" Helen asked.

"I wonder what makes a person decide to climb through their girlfriend's mother's window and bite her? How could he possibly have thought that was a good idea?" It was a rhetorical question, of course.

As Helen was backing our rig into the building, the police radio suddenly exploded with activity. "Suspect is in the house! Repeat: Suspect is in the house! Suspect is attacking the victim!"

Helen and I looked at each other in horror. "I hope Mrs. Schuster's okay!" we both said in unison. To be attacked once is terrible, but twice in the same night is unimaginable! *Jesus, please protect Mrs. Schuster from Stephen.*

We stayed at the building, glued to the police radio. Less than ten minutes later, we were dispatched for another first aid call.

DISPATCHER: "Request for first aid at police headquarters for a medical emergency."

"Wow!" I exclaimed. "I hope one of the police didn't get injured by Stephen."

"This is getting stranger by the minute," Helen replied. "I wonder what's going on."

Helen pulled the ambulance back onto the road. Police headquarters was only three blocks away. She pulled behind the police station and we went in the rear entrance, where they bring in the prisoners.

I hadn't seen Stephen in at least ten years, but I recognized him right away. Dirty-blond hair was held back loosely in a haphazard pony tail. He had a streak of dirt on his right cheek. He sat hunched over on a bench in the holding area and stared morosely at the floor, his left foot nervously tapping against the hard concrete.

How did he end up in this mess? Why on earth did he do what he did? I supposed that we would probably never really understand why.

"We called you to take a look at Stephen because he's complaining of a headache," Officer Endicott explained.

Yeah, right. He's probably just trying to delay going to jail.

Helen pulled Officer Endicott aside. "So, what happened after we left?" she whispered.

"Somehow, Stephen managed to sneak back into the house," he said.

"When exactly?" Helen asked, her eyes widening with surprise.

"I'm going to guess right after we searched it."

"Where was he hiding?" I asked. Part of me wanted to know the answer, and another part of me didn't.

"In the closet," Officer Endicott replied.

I choked on my spit. *In the closet?! Did I just hear correctly? Did he just say that Stephen was in the closet? That he was hiding just a few feet away from us the entire time?* A chill raced down my spine.

"What did you just say?" Helen asked. "In the closet? As in, he was there the whole time that we were in there?"

"Yeah, really sorry about that. Like I said, he somehow must have slipped back in after we searched the house," he said sheepishly.

Stephen was watching us and listening to us the entire time we took care of Janet! Thank God he didn't surprise us from behind with a knife! It's something that volunteers don't usually think about when responding to an emergency call, but sometimes we may find ourselves in dangerous situations. And not even know it. *This time, Helen and I got lucky. Thank You, Lord, for keeping Mrs. Schuster, Helen, and me safe tonight.*

I jumped when Stephen suddenly leaned back hard on the bench. He fixed his gaze on Helen and me. I tried not to squirm. I didn't think he recognized me and I was glad.

"Why don't you grab a pressure," Helen suggested.

"Gee, thanks." I grabbed our blood pressure cuff and sat on the bench next to Stephen. I got straight to the point. "Is anything bothering you?" I asked him.

Stephen ignored me. Instead, he sullenly stared straight ahead. I didn't see the point of trying to make small talk with him. I figured that he was lost in his own thoughts. Or maybe I was wrong. Maybe he recognized me after all and was now embarrassed. I hoped it was the former.

"Blood pressure and pulse are okay," I said to Helen, who was filling out the run sheet. I quickly checked Stephen over for injuries. In the end, we didn't transport him to the hospital. Stephen appeared destined to spend the night in the county jail.

"Well, that's one relationship that's probably going to bite the dust tonight," I remarked to Helen, as we were climbing back into our ambulance. "No pun intended." After all, if your boyfriend breaks into your house and bites your mother's finger, that's probably a red flag.

Guardian Angel in Action

*Heal me, LORD, and I will be healed; save me and
I will be saved, for you are the one I praise.*

JEREMIAH 17:14

I t was a little before two o'clock in the morning, and I was just coming off the night shift as a beach cop. It was a busy night: We confiscated fireworks from a man hiding with his son under one of the lifeguard stands, helped a motorist who locked his keys in his car, and investigated a report of several teenagers getting amorous at the "Underwood Motel." (Yes, you guessed it—that would be underneath our boardwalk.)

I placed my radio in its charger and then stopped in the dispatch room to say hello to Jerome Franklin. Jerome glanced up and nodded to me. "I'm about to tap you out for a call," he said.

I grumbled an unintelligible response. *So much for going to bed.* I stepped out of the dispatch room so that my pager wouldn't cause feedback during the transmission.

DISPATCHER: "Request for mutual aid at Mulligan's Tavern for six pedestrians struck."

The call was in a neighboring town directly in front of the local bar. "It's a hit-and-run," Jerome explained to me. "We're looking for a white pickup truck."

"Okay," I said. I was dragging, but of course I wanted to go. I guess that's human nature. I hopped into the driver's seat of one ambulance and drove over with Colleen and Alec. A second crew took the other ambulance.

Alec whistled softly. "Wow, what a nightmare," he said as we pulled up close to Mulligan's Tavern.

The scene seemed chaotic at first glance. Closing time for the local bars is two o'clock, so many pedestrians were wandering (and, in some instances, staggering) around. *No wonder so many people got hit,* I thought.

I glanced around before I stepped out of the ambulance. The police had blocked the road to traffic, which was helpful. I saw two young women in their twenties lying on the sidewalk, fairly close to our ambulance. Both were rummaging in their purses. The women looked like they had some minor cuts and scrapes, but nothing too bad. A large man with a long brown beard sat about ten feet away. He was rocking back and forth, clutching his left ankle. Yet another man was lying near the curb, rubbing his right shoulder. It looked as though there might be another victim or two in the road, but it was hard to tell with the crowd. The patients I could see looked like they mainly had abrasions, lacerations, and orthopedic injuries.

Buzz Bernard, a competent EMT who was the captain of a neighboring squad, came over to give us our assignment. Buzz pointed to the male victim sitting on the sidewalk. "He said the truck hit him while he was standing in front of the bar, waiting for a cab. Can you take care of him?"

"Of course," Colleen answered. "We're on it."

Dodging drunken pedestrians, our trio walked over to the man Buzz had assigned to us. "Hello, sir. I'm Alec, and this is Colleen and Andrea. We're members of the Pine Cove First Aid Squad. We heard that you got hit by a truck. What's your name and how are you feeling?"

"Name's Snake and I feel lousy," he grunted.

Snake had an eclectic mixture of tattoos of lizards, snakes, and cartoon characters covering much of his exposed areas. Maybe Alec should have asked him, "What's your birth name?" Although Snake smelled of liquor, he seemed to be sobering up in a hurry.

"Can you tell us what happened?" Colleen asked him.

"He plowed straight into us, and then he just took off," Snake answered. "I wish I could get my hands on that guy…" He shook a beefy fist in the air to accentuate his point. *I'm glad that Snake doesn't have a quarrel with me!*

"What's hurting you?" Colleen asked him.

"My neck, back, and ankle," he replied. "Mainly my ankle. It feels like it's busted. I can't put no weight on it."

Colleen and Alec immobilized Snake's neck with a collar, and then Alec and I splinted Snake's ankle with a pillow. Colleen gave him a little bit of oxygen via a nasal cannula, and then we placed him on a backboard.

After we loaded Snake into the rig, paramedics Baxter and Roberta arrived. Baxter stepped up into our ambulance, and Roberta went to check on the other victims. I climbed into the driver's seat and waited for the go-ahead to roll.

"You can go," Baxter called up front to me. "I'll do the IV line on the way." I looked in my rearview mirror and saw Colleen climb out. I figured she was going to drive the medic's rig.

One of our police officers, Brad Sims, tapped on my driver's window. "I'm going to give you a police escort," he said.

"Okay," I said. "Lead the way." I had no idea why I was getting a police escort. I had never had one before, and I wasn't quite sure of the purpose. But at the time I didn't question it. I'm a pretty low-key person and tend to just roll with things. I checked my side-view mirror and saw that Colleen was indeed in the medic's rig. She gave me a thumbs-up, indicating that she was ready to follow.

Following Officer Sims' lead, I flipped on my lights and sirens. The roads were practically deserted; I passed two cabs and one minivan in the first four miles. *Only one mile to go.*

As we neared the hospital, Officer Sims peeled off and let me take the lead. *I guess he has to go back to the accident scene*, I thought. I focused on the road ahead.

About two hundred feet later, I approached a large multilane intersection which was just a few blocks from the hospital. I flicked on my left turn signal. *Green light. Good, no one's coming from the north. I'm clear to make my turn.*

And then, for some unknown reason, even though I had a green light, I slowed down and came to a complete stop. When I reflect back on that night, I believe my guardian angel must have been sitting in the seat next to me, telling me to stop the ambulance.

Just as I came to a stop, two police cars blew through the red light at a tremendous speed, travelling west on the intersecting road. Since they had their own sirens blaring, they did not hear mine.

Temporarily stunned, I felt myself trembling with shock, relief, and a host of other emotions. If one of those township police cars had struck the side of our ambulance, it would surely have flipped us. Alec and Baxter weren't even wearing seatbelts. If I had simply rolled through the green light without stopping, one or both of those police officers would likely have expired. In addition, Alec, Baxter, and Snake could have died as well. Maybe even me. And if Officer Sims hadn't turned off when he did, he could have been injured or killed as well. It was the closest I have ever come to having an accident while driving the ambulance. I was shaken to the core.

To this day, when I turn left at that particular intersection, I recall the near-miss. *Thank you, guardian angel, for being by my side and protecting me and my crew. Thank You, God, for keeping us all safe.*

Getting Too Worked Up

When Jesus landed and saw a large crowd, he
had compassion on them and healed their sick.

MATTHEW 14:14

Kurt Schultz could practically feel his blood pressure rising as he listened to a local businessman propose a plan to rezone the land directly across the street from his home from residential to commercial. His front window looked out on a beautiful open field. He loved watching the local wildlife enjoy the "little patch of green," as he liked to call it. His street was very quiet, and he wanted to keep it that way. *A business will absolutely destroy our little street.*

"This is terrible," Kurt whispered to his older brother, Anton. The two brothers had lived together for the past ten years, since Anton became a widower. "I need to stand up and say something." The town council meeting room was packed with local residents, many of whom were displeased about the business proposal.

"Okay, but Kurt, you need to take a deep breath first," Anton said. "You're getting too upset. Your face is turning very red."

"Of course my face is turning red," Kurt replied. "You know that my face always turns red when I'm spitting mad!"

The Pine Cove mayor, an older gentleman who had been on the town council for the past five years, gently tapped his gavel. "We will now accept public comments regarding the proposal," he said.

Kurt immediately stood up. "Kurt Schultz, 54 Waverly Drive. I would like to state for the record that I am adamantly opposed to this half-cooked proposal for a multitude of reasons!" Kurt stated his objections with gusto until finally Anton gently tugged his arm to sit back down.

"I think you made your point loud and clear, Kurt. Give someone else a chance," he said softly. "You're getting yourself too worked up."

Kurt sank back down into his seat. He tried to focus on what the other residents were saying, but he was distracted by an odd sensation in his chest. *Maybe Anton was right. I am getting too worked up. I feel like I have a big fish flopping around in my chest.*

Kurt turned to his brother. "I said my piece. I think I'd like to go home now." *Maybe if I go home and lie down, this terrible feeling will go away.*

....

DISPATCHER: "Request for first aid at 54 Waverly Drive for a 74-year-old male with a medical emergency."

When Mason, Dillon, and I arrived at Waverly Drive, we found two older men seated at a rustic oak table in a small kitchen. I could tell right away which of the two was our patient, because he was leaning forward, resting his head in his hands. Rivulets of sweat coursed down his cheeks.

The other gentleman, who had a head full of thick, white hair, stood up to introduce himself. "I'm Anton Schultz, and this is my brother, Kurt. We just came home from the town council meeting. While we were there, Kurt got very upset. He got so upset we had to come home." Anton, who had a sturdy build despite his advanced years, patted his brother on his back.

Kurt raised his head briefly and moaned, "My heart is racing. I feel terrible."

I sat down next to Kurt and tried to check his pulse. "It's so weak and rapid that I can't really count it accurately," I said. I placed the back of my hand on his forehead. It felt cool and clammy to the touch.

Dillon handed me a blood pressure cuff. I tried to take Kurt's blood pressure, but I couldn't hear anything with the stethoscope. When I tried again, I was able to get a systolic pressure of 80 by palpation. A normal systolic pressure is about 120. *Too low.*

Dillon hooked Kurt up to our heart monitor. "His pulse is 260," he whispered discreetly, so as not to frighten Kurt even more than he already was. Since a resting heart rate should be between 60 and 100, we knew Kurt was in tachycardia. His body would not be able to withstand such a high pulse coupled with such a low blood pressure indefinitely.

"Medics are here," Mason said, glancing out the window. "Looks like Ty and Paula. I'm going to go outside and tell them what we've got," he added, closing the front door behind him.

After Dillon placed Kurt on oxygen, we assisted him from the kitchen chair to our stretcher. I picked up our clipboard and began writing up our call sheet.

"Anton, does Kurt have any medical problems?" I asked.

"Yes, he had a heart attack two years ago and got a stent. He also has high blood pressure and high cholesterol," he answered.

When Ty stepped inside, he immediately switched Kurt over to his own heart monitor. "You're right about the heart rate," he commented to us. "He's in ventricular tachycardia."

Left untreated, ventricular tachycardia can lead to ventricular fibrillation and death. It was a good thing Kurt's brother called us when he did.

"Kurt, I'm going to start an IV line and try to slow down your heart with medication," Paula said. She tied a rubber tourniquet around his upper arm.

A few minutes after receiving the medication, Kurt said, "I still feel terrible. I think I'm going to faint." He looked even paler than he had when we first came in.

"Kurt, I'm afraid the medication isn't doing the job. We're going to have to give your heart a little shock," Paula said.

"Shock my heart? With what? Will it hurt?" Kurt asked.

"We're going to use a defibrillator. It will be painful, but we're going to give you some morphine to make it more comfortable," Paula explained.

At the time, I didn't realize that conscious people could be defibrillated. I thought defibrillators were strictly for patients in cardiac arrest. However, the medics possess the ability to shock at a lower level of power than that administered by semiautomatic defibrillators. This enables them to restore patients in tachycardia to a normal sinus rhythm. *Dear Lord, I really hope this works.*

I could see that Kurt was becoming more and more anxious. "My chest is starting to hurt," he said. A bead of sweat hung briefly from his chin before dripping onto his chest.

"That's because your heart is beating too fast," Ty replied as he attached pads to Kurt's chest. "We really need to slow it down a bit."

Anton paced nervously back and forth in the kitchen. "Kurt, it'll be okay," he said. I got the feeling that Anton said this as much to try to convince himself as to convince Kurt. I tried to console Kurt by patting his shoulder, but stopped when Ty told us to clear the patient. Without delay, Ty pressed the shock button. Kurt let out a yell that made the hair on the back of my neck stand at full attention. *Wow—I sure hope that shock did the trick! I'm not sure if he could stand another!*

Kurt continued moaning. The morphine didn't seem like it did much. "What happened?" he asked.

"We were able to convert you to a normal heart rhythm," Ty replied. "You should start to feel better now."

Unfortunately, no sooner had Ty spoken than Kurt slipped back into ventricular tachycardia. I glanced at the heart monitor; his heart rate was about 250.

"Oh no, the feeling's coming back again. I feel so terrible," Kurt said. "I'm going to pass out. Please, do something."

"Sorry, Kurt," Ty said. "I'm afraid we're going to have to shock you again."

"Do what?" Kurt said. "Shock me? Will it hurt?" He apparently did not remember the first shock anymore. *I guess the morphine is working after all*. I gave him another pat on the shoulder before stepping back out of the way.

Ty shocked Kurt again, and once again Kurt let out a cry. Anton flinched. This time, however, Kurt stayed in a normal sinus rhythm. *Thank You, God, for walking by Kurt's side throughout this emergency.*

After a few minutes, Kurt started to feel better. "The chest pain is gone," he said. At that point, we loaded Kurt into the ambulance and transported him to Bakersville Hospital. Anton later told us that Kurt spent a few days in the cardiac intensive care unit and received a pacemaker. Kurt made a full recovery, but I'm not sure if he went back to any more of our town council meetings!

The Attempted Murder

Help us, God our Savior, for the glory of your name;
deliver us and forgive our sins for your name's sake.

PSALM 79:9

Late one chilly January evening, Arthur Peters calmly rang the doorbell of his former home on a prestigious street in a town that borders my own. Mr. Peters, an accountant, had moved out in June. Since then, he had been living in an apartment complex in our town. His wife, Amy, continued to reside at the residence with their two children, Terrence and Jordan.

Amy, an attractive woman in her early fifties, cracked the front door open. "What do you want, Arthur?" she asked with a sigh. He had already called several times earlier that day. Amy felt like he was just trying to bait her into an argument, and she truly wasn't in the mood to fight anymore. She just wanted peace. Peace, and to finalize the divorce. She had filed for divorce in August and was counting the days until it became finalized.

And now Arthur stood on the front porch, holding a small wooden box in his hands. "I need to go over some papers with you," he said. "Please open the door."

Almost reluctantly, Amy stepped aside and let him in. *Remember, he's the father of your children. Let him have his say and get it over with.* She knew he wouldn't leave until he got his own way.

Amy caught a flash of steel out of the corner of her eye. *Dear Lord, please tell me he does not have a gun. Please tell me that he is not here to kill me. To kill Terrence. To kill Jordan.* Amy looked more closely. And there it was. A pistol in the waistband of her estranged husband's pants! *Since when does Arthur own a gun?* Ever so slowly, so as not to draw his attention, she eased closer to the kitchen counter. Briefly, she gazed up at her children, a look of terror in her eyes. Then, without hesitation, Amy pressed the small red button which she knew would activate her audible security alarm system.

"Did you just do that?" Arthur asked Amy, his voice shaking with anger. "Did you just set off the alarm?"

"Yes," Amy replied, a quiver of fear evident in her voice. *Please don't let me die like this. Please don't kill my children.*

"Then you're dead," he replied, pulling the gun from his waistband and aiming it at Amy's chest.

"Please, no," Amy whimpered. Despite Amy's plea, Arthur Peters pulled the trigger. The haunting sound of a gunshot pierced the night air.

"No!" Terrence cried, leaping in front of his mother, attempting to shield her from the bullet. To shield his mother from the man to whom she had been married for 27 years. To shield her from his own father.

The first bullet struck Amy square in the chest. Amy collapsed to the ground, her head hitting the ceramic tile floor with a loud thud. She placed one hand over her chest and felt something warm and sticky. *Am I going to die?* Slowly, everything turned to blackness.

The next bullet struck Terrence in the left arm. Terrence landed hard on the kitchen floor near his mother, and he quickly rolled to cover her body with his own.

Once again, Arthur Peters aimed the gun at his wife and fired. Mercifully, the third shot missed, instead ricocheting off a kitchen cabinet. Jordan, briefly paralyzed with shock and horror, quickly came to her senses. Mustering up her strength and courage, she charged her father. She tackled him to the ground and a wild scuffle ensued. As Jordan and Arthur wrestled, Terrence dragged himself from the floor and jumped on top of them. Together, the siblings joined in a life-and-death struggle against their father.

Breaking loose, Jordan crawled along the floor and kicked the pistol out of her father's reach. Then she and her brother held their father down, praying that the police would arrive soon.

"Is Mom breathing?" Terrence asked his sister, fearing the worst.

"I can't tell," Jordan answered, half-sobbing. "Mom, are you okay? Can you hear me?"

But Amy lay motionless on the floor, unresponsive. Crimson blood pooled underneath where she lay. Suddenly, there was heavy banging on the front door. "Open up! Police!"

"Help us!" Terrence cried out. "My mom needs help!"

The officers promptly broke the door down and radioed for medical assistance.

DISPATCHER: *"Request for mutual aid for two gunshot victims."*

The only gunshot calls I have responded to have been self-inflicted. This certainly did not sound like one of those types of calls. Helen, Buddy, Ted, and I hurried to the scene.

"Stay in your rig," Dispatcher Jerome Franklin said. "An officer will come out to meet you."

"Received," Helen said. She parked our ambulance outside a beautiful two-story brick residence and awaited further instructions. Several of our town's police cars also responded to the call to assist. Officer Sims met us at our ambulance and briefly filled us in on what had just transpired. "We want you to stage here and be ready to back up the primary squad if they need more help," he explained.

I watched out the side window of our ambulance, trying to figure out what was going on. I noticed Officer Sims was now surrounding the house with yellow crime scene tape. Several detectives from the sheriff's office arrived and began conversing with him.

Within a few minutes, the volunteer squad members, along with a team of paramedics, wheeled Amy Peters outside. It was difficult to see in the dark, but she appeared to be intubated. I prayed that her injuries would not prove to be fatal.

A minute later or so, Terrence was carried out by rescue personnel. It looked like his arm was heavily bandaged. I was glad to see he was alert and talking.

Next, a man whom I presumed to be Arthur Peters, was escorted outside by two police officers. As he walked past our ambulance, I could see that a pair of handcuffs bound his hands together. I watched as he was placed in the back of a patrol car. Seconds later, he was driven away into the darkness. *What on earth makes a person take such a drastic step as to shoot other human beings?*

Meanwhile, two ambulances, with their lights flashing, disappeared into the darkness with Amy and Terrence. We continued to stand by at the scene, and after about five minutes, our squad was dispatched for an additional call.

> **DISPATCHER:** "Request for mutual aid at the police department for high blood pressure."

"Let's go!" Ted said. "We're ready."

"We're in service," Helen told Jerome, heading toward the police department.

"Do you think the call is for the shooter?" I asked. "He must have just arrived at headquarters."

"It wouldn't be surprising if he has high blood pressure after what he just did," Buddy said.

We proceeded a few blocks to the police department and Helen parked out front. Security seemed especially tight tonight. Our first aid team was buzzed through to the holding area.

Our patient was indeed Arthur Peters. He sat on a hard bench inside a holding cell. I noticed that sweat was dripping from his bald head and landing on his beige trousers. His skin was a sickly shade of pasty white. *I suppose that he's gradually realizing that he's in a ton of trouble.*

Colt Lewis, a veteran detective from the county sheriff's department, was questioning Arthur. "And what did you do today after you picked up your gun permit from the Pine Cove Police Department?" he asked.

"I bought a 9mm and then went to the driving range to practice," Arthur whispered, pushing his glasses up higher on his nose.

"And then…" Detective Lewis prompted.

"I drove straight to our home," Arthur said. At that point, Arthur clammed up. He glanced up at us. "I think I need a lawyer."

Detective Lewis stepped back. "Thank you for coming out tonight," he said to us. "Mr. Peters is complaining of high blood pressure. Would you mind checking it for us?"

"No problem," Buddy said, grabbing our cuff from our kit.

It felt very strange to me to be assisting the very man who had just caused so much heartache and injury. His complaint of high blood pressure seemed so paltry in comparison to his estranged wife's injuries. But then I reminded myself I was not called here tonight to be this man's judge. *That particular duty lies with a much higher power.*

Arthur's blood pressure was high, but not really *that* high, considering. In the end, we didn't transport him to the hospital. Instead, the police processed him and brought him to the county jail.

Fortunately, the bullet that struck Terrence Peters did not do any serious damage and he was released from Bakersville Hospital the next day. His mother remained in critical condition for five days, after which time she was upgraded to fair condition. I was less certain as to Arthur Peter's future. One thing I knew for sure: his life as he knew it was about to change drastically.

The efforts of Terrence and Jordan were nothing short of heroic. The two siblings joined together that night to save their mother's life. By the grace of God, the three survived.

Baby, Baby

*Even while the boy was coming, the demon threw him to
the ground in a convulsion. But Jesus rebuked the impure
spirit, healed the boy and gave him back to his father.*

LUKE 9:42

Sometimes, babies never even have a chance and we never know why.
The evening before, we had been summoned to police headquarters
for a maternity call. We found our patient, a beautiful young woman
who was six months pregnant, sobbing hysterically in the front seat of
a light blue minivan parked directly in front of the police station. She
and her husband were driving home from the movies when she began
experiencing severe pain and abdominal cramping. Her husband drove
directly to the police station. The poor woman miscarried right then
and there. Sudden, unexpected, brutal. A devastating end to the prospective parents' dream.

> **DISPATCHER:** "Expedite: Request for first aid at 111 Chestnut Street
> for a baby who is not breathing and is turning blue."

And so now, less than twelve hours later, I found myself in the
ambulance on the way to another call for a baby in distress. I still felt
unsettled from the previous call; witnessing the young couple's anguish
had been heartbreaking. *I hope this call has a happier ending.*

"Grab the infant kit," Alec directed. We have a separate pediatric kit that holds supplies for infants and children: small ambu bags, oxygen masks, and blood pressure cuffs for the pint-sized crowd. I grabbed the small orange kit and followed Alec and Colleen up the walkway toward a white house with blue shutters.

As I approached the house, I could already hear screaming and shouting. Sergeant Derrick Flint rushed out the front door and came hurrying toward us, cradling a small infant in his arms. As he dodged a variety of toddler toys that cluttered the walk, he reminded me of a linebacker trying to complete a football play. As he approached the ambulance, I quickly opened the side door. "This is the Ritchies' two-month-old infant," he said, handing the baby to Alec. "Bobby didn't sleep well last night. When Mrs. Ritchie checked on him this morning, he had a high fever."

A sobbing mother and distraught father trailed immediately behind Sergeant Flint. The Ritchies' terror was almost palpable. Mrs. Ritchie was dressed in pajamas and a robe, with fuzzy animal slippers on her feet. Her husband wore sweatpants and a rumpled white T-shirt. They both looked like they had already had a long night.

Alec and I quickly strapped the baby into an infant seat, which was mounted to our stretcher. Colleen set up blow-by oxygen with a pediatric mask.

"Do something!" Mr. Ritchie bellowed. "Why don't you do something?"

The infant was convulsing; frightening seizures consumed his tiny body. His face was very blue; definitely not the color any parent ever envisions for his or her child. *God, please help us care for this innocent child of Yours.*

"Please tell us what's going on," Alec said, ignoring Mr. Ritchie's confrontational tone. "When exactly did this start?"

"Bobby had a fever last night, so I gave him some Tylenol. He cried on and off all night. This morning, he felt warm again, so I took his temperature," Mrs. Ritchie managed to explain in between sobs. "It was 106 degrees! The next thing I knew, he was shaking all over. I think for a few seconds he stopped breathing."

"We called 911 right away," Mr. Ritchie added. "Are you helping him?" He began pounding his fist against the side wall of our ambulance. "I said I want you to help him!"

It was easy to see that Bobby's father was starting to melt down from the stress. I was starting to grow concerned that he was going to damage our ambulance. I also didn't want him to decide it was okay to start punching one of us like that.

Mr. Ritchie's behavior distracted me and put me on edge. Our policy is to allow one parent to ride in the back of the ambulance with us. The other can ride in the front seat of the ambulance or drive his or her own car. As far as I was concerned, Mrs. Ritchie could stay but it was time for her husband to go.

"I said *do something!*" Bobby's father hollered, and he looked as though he was about to shove Alec into one of the side cabinets of the ambulance.

We had had enough. I opened up the side door and called out to Sergeant Flint, "We need help in here." Mr. Ritchie's behavior was too wild, creating an unsafe scene for us as well as the baby.

"Okay there, Mr. Ritchie. I'm going to need you to step outside and give them some room to work," Sergeant Flint said. His tone left no room for an argument. He placed one large hand on Mr. Ritchie's shoulder and escorted him out of the ambulance.

I breathed a sigh of relief and refocused my attention on Bobby. He was still struggling to breathe. Colleen, who continued to provide Bobby with oxygen with a pediatric mask held close to his face, made sure his airway remained open. I placed several cold packs on his body in an attempt to bring his temperature down. Bobby's mother clutched one of his tiny hands within her own.

"The medics aren't available," Alec said. "I'm going to start driving." Very gradually, while we were travelling to the hospital, Bobby's limbs quieted. *Thank You, Lord, for taking care of Bobby.*

"His color's much better now," Colleen said as the frightening blue faded away. Bobby began to cry, and his small face now changed to a welcome shade of red. *I don't think I've ever been so glad to hear a baby cry.*

The unborn infant from the call the previous evening would never have a chance to cry in this world. But Bobby made a full recovery; he would live to see many more days.

. . . .

Many emergency medical technicians hope that they will one day deliver a baby. Part of me would absolutely love to deliver a baby. However, the other part of me worries *what if?* As in, what if something terrible goes wrong? What if the baby isn't breathing? What if the baby is born with a low Apgar score? EMTs are trained to handle routine deliveries. Complications are most certainly better handled on the obstetrical floor of the hospital than in the back of an ambulance.

DISPATCHER: "Request 1005 Hanover Road for a maternity call."

"I heard on the scanner that she's 38 weeks pregnant," Chris Nicholson said excitedly on the way to the scene.

The call was at a sprawling ranch on a corner property a few blocks from the beach. We entered the home through a side door, near the attached garage.

"Boys, please wait out in the hall for a minute," Helen said, smiling at Mason and Chris. "Andrea, you come with me."

Helen and I stepped into the master bedroom. Our patient, Jane, sat perched on the edge of her bed. She was a pretty young woman with long brown hair tied back in a ponytail. A packed suitcase lay open on the floor next to her. Her husband hovered close by. "My husband was going to drive me, but…" Jane paused mid-sentence, doubling over with pain.

"No explanation necessary," Helen said. "It looks like your contractions are coming pretty close together." It would be downright risky for Jane to try driving with her husband at this point, unless she wanted him to deliver her baby in the car. *That certainly wouldn't be my first choice.*

"Did your water break yet?" I asked.

"Yes, a short while ago," Jane replied. "I saw the bloody show too," she added. A bead of sweat trickled slowly down her cheek.

I timed her contractions. They were about one minute apart.

"Is this your first child?" Helen asked, wiping Jane's forehead with a cloth.

"No, my second." Second deliveries can occur much more rapidly than first ones. My guess was that Jane's baby would probably be making an appearance in this world *very* soon.

"I want to go to Randolph Medical Center," Jane said firmly. "My doctor's there."

"Randolph's pretty far," I said doubtfully. It was a solid thirty-minute drive without traffic. I didn't think we had thirty minutes. "We should go to Bakersville…it's much closer," I suggested.

"We should definitely go to Bakersville," Helen agreed. "Unless, of course, you want us to be the ones delivering your baby." Although Helen was joking, Jane took her offer seriously.

"Okay, you two can deliver it for me. I *really* want to go to Randolph, so I'm okay with taking the chance," Jane said. "By the way, how many babies have you delivered?"

"You mean between the two of us?" I asked.

Jane nodded her head.

I couldn't help smiling. "Not a one," I replied cheerfully.

Jane smiled back. "Okay, then maybe Bakersville it is after all," she laughed.

We made Jane as comfortable as possible on our stretcher. She was sweating profusely now. The contractions were now coming every forty-five seconds.

We rolled with lights and sirens to the hospital. "Dispatch," Mason, our driver, said, "We need you to call ahead to the hospital. Have someone meet us at the front door. We're going to need to go straight to maternity."

I carefully set up our maternity kit: sterile exam gloves, sterile umbilical clamps, a draping sheet, scissors, obstetrical wipes, alcohol preps, sterile gauze, obstetrical pads, a sterile bulb syringe, and a receiving blanket.

Helen mopped Jane's face with a moist cloth. We encouraged her to pace her breathing. "I think he's coming," she panted.

"I'm sure you're right," I said, "but we're pulling up to the hospital now. It would be better if you could wait just one more minute."

Jane moaned with each contraction. They were practically one on top of the next at this point. We quickly wheeled Jane into the hospital's front foyer.

"I've got the elevator ready for you," an elderly security guard said, smiling. We rolled in and whisked Jane to the third floor.

The unit secretary, a tall woman with a very large bun on the very top of her head, buzzed us in. "Room four," she directed, pointing to the left.

"I'm telling you, he's coming!" Jane cried out.

A physician and team of nurses met us there. Quickly, they helped us slide Jane from our stretcher to theirs. I took one last look and could see the baby's head crowning! Then I stepped away from Jane's bedside to give the doctor room to work.

One of the maternity nurses pulled the curtain closed. At that precise moment, I heard the robust cry of a newborn baby. Helen's and my faces lit up with smiles. *What greater blessing is there than to witness the birth of a new child?*

"It's a boy!" I heard the nurse say.

We could have agreed to let Jane go to Randolph Hospital and Helen and I would have delivered our very first baby. But I felt like we made the right decision. We played it safe. I have no regrets.

It's been many years and I've answered at least 5,000 calls since that night. So you might wonder at this point, how many babies have Helen and I delivered? Still zero, but who's counting?

....

A few months later, Meg and I were standing by at a 5K run in a neighboring town.

"Wow, these runners are really struggling," I said. I took a sip of ice-cold water.

"Yes, it's so hot and humid today," Meg replied. It was half past eleven, and the thermometer was already pushing 95 degrees.

Just after the last runner passed us by, we were dispatched to respond to a first aid call.

DISPATCHER: "Request for first aid at the Wesley Avenue Beach for an infant with heatstroke."

Meg and I drove straight over to the beach and met Alec and Colleen at the scene. When I stepped out of the rig, I felt like I was stepping directly into a blazing furnace. There was absolutely no sea breeze—just pure, oppressive heat. The thermometer had climbed to 102 degrees.

Our patient was Madeline, a redheaded three-month-old infant. Her cheeks appeared cherry red and I could see that she was no longer sweating. Madeline's mother held her in her arms and her father stood anxiously close by. Both parents appeared to be in shock.

"We need to get her under the shower right away," Colleen said, quickly taking Madeline in her arms. She began dousing Madeline with cool water in order to bring down her core body temperature. I prepared several cold packs for the trip to the hospital.

Heatstroke is a true, life-threatening medical emergency caused by excessive exposure to the sun (high temperatures) or by overexertion in hot conditions. When the core body temperature reaches 104 degrees or higher, one is considered to have heatstroke. Young children and older adults are at the greatest risk for developing the condition.

"Could you tell us what's happening with Madeline this morning?" Meg asked her parents.

"We got here about three hours ago," Madeline's mother said worriedly. "I kept her under the umbrella the whole time and she's been drinking some formula, but…"

"We noticed she started getting listless and hot to the touch…" Madeline's father said.

"So we called 911," the mother finished.

If untreated, heatstroke can damage the brain, heart, kidneys, and muscles. Cooling Madeline down was urgent. After several minutes under the shower, Madeline's skin gradually began to feel a little cooler to the touch. *I hope that means her internal organs are cooling off too.*

Colleen carefully placed Madeline in an infant seat on top of our stretcher. We carefully placed cold packs in her armpits, her groin, and behind her neck.

"We need to get moving," Alec said. For most calls, we don't need to use lights and sirens when traveling to the hospital. However, this case constituted a true emergency; every minute counted.

The pediatric team met us at the emergency room doors and brought Madeline directly into a treatment room. We had done our part. *Madeline's in good hands now. Please keep watching over her, Lord.*

I ran into Madeline's parents a few weeks later and learned that she made a full recovery. "From now on, we plan to leave her home with a sitter instead of bringing her to the beach," her mother said.

The Birthday Cruise

*Answer me when I call to you, my righteous
God. Give me relief from my distress; have
mercy on me and hear my prayer.*

PSALM 4:1

Tyler Vandenburg's birthday party cruise wasn't going as planned. He had turned 22 years old today, and had planned a special four-hour cruise with five of his closest friends. They just wanted to kick back, relax, and enjoy some pleasant time at sea. However, the weather wasn't cooperating with their plans. For a summer day it was downright chilly, and now the wind was really picking up. *I wonder if there's a gale force warning in effect. Maybe we should turn back early.*

Tyler's friend Darlene tapped him on the shoulder, interrupting his thoughts. "Tyler, I don't know much about boating, but isn't that jetty getting awfully close to our boat?"

Tyler spun around and looked in the direction that Darlene was pointing. "I think you're right. We're definitely getting too close." *I wish I had a little more experience taking the boat out without my dad to help. What would he do in this situation? Well, he probably wouldn't have gotten himself into this situation in the first place.* "I'm going to try to turn us around."

"Okay, Tyler. I'm going to go grab our life jackets. Maybe we should put them on," Darlene suggested.

"Good idea," Tyler said. "Better do it fast. I'm really struggling with the wheel and the waves are suddenly getting a lot bigger."

Darlene disappeared from sight around the side of the boat. Tyler blinked as ocean water sprayed him in the face. *Tyler, man, you are totally losing control of this situation. If you don't do something fast, you're totally going to smack into that jetty!*

Suddenly, a large wave crashed over the boat, propelling it dangerously close to the jetty. "Guys, we need to get off this boat right now!" Tyler shouted. "We need to jump!"

"We don't have the life vests on yet!" Darlene called from down below.

With that, the boat struck hard against the jetty. Although he tried to hold on, Tyler was thrown from the boat and into the cold ocean water. As his head went underwater, he could hear his friends screaming. *Dear Lord, please help us!*

....

"I'm home," I called, shivering as I peeled off my beach patrol windbreaker. I felt like the damp, chilly ocean air had seeped deep into my bones during my eight-hour shift as a special officer. It hadn't been much of a beach day; in fact, the cold, cloudy and windy weather had kept most prospective beachgoers far away.

"Great, sweetie," my mom said, stirring a pot of homemade Manhattan clam chowder. "Dinner will be ready in five."

"Thanks!" I replied. But just as I was about to sneak a taste of the soup, my pager went off.

You have got to be kidding me! Reluctantly, I put the spoon down. The soup would have to wait. *At least I know Mom will keep it hot for me.*

DISPATCHER: "Request for first aid for a boat that has crashed into the Wesley Avenue Jetty. Seven or eight people are in the water."

The call was at the southern end of town. We rolled all three ambulances; with eight victims, we would need all three and maybe even some more from neighboring towns.

"Still in your uniform?" Dillon asked as we headed toward the scene in the ambulance.

"Yeah, I just got home. I wish I'd had a few minutes to put on something warmer first. It's freezing at the beach."

Dillon handed me a pile of blankets to carry down to the water. *Too bad one of these isn't for me.* As I stepped out of the rig, the damp salty air whipped back my hair and struck me full upon my face. For every two steps I took forward, I felt like the blustery wind was blowing me one step back. Dillon, Colleen, Ted, Sadie Martinez, Buddy, and I struggled along the path that wound through the dunes and down onto the beach.

Because it was such a cold and raw afternoon, the beach was empty except for the police and lifeguards. Sergeant Flint and Officer McGovern stood side by side at the water's edge.

"Help!" I heard a voice shout from the ocean. "Over here!"

A young woman was standing precariously on what was left of the boat. The boat was slamming hard against the unforgiving jetty.

"You need to jump!" Officer McGovern shouted, cupping his hands close to his mouth so his voice would carry. "JUMP!"

"We're coming to get you! Jump and swim away from the jetty!" a lifeguard shouted. Holding a torpedo buoy attached to a rope, she rushed into the water and began swimming toward the boat. The other guards held the line, ready to pull the victim to safety.

Clearly terrified, the young woman teetered back and forth for a moment, and then finally jumped. She tried her best to swim away from the jetty, but the pounding waves had different ideas.

Meanwhile, another of the victims in the water cried out, "Over here!" Although he was treading water, he appeared to be fatiguing.

Another guard swam out toward the young man in the water. "You're going to be okay," the guard called to him. "I'll be with you in a second!"

I held my breath as the lifeguards began pulling the two victims to safety. *Dear Lord, please be with the lifeguards during this rescue and let them save the swimmers!*

My eyes swept across the shoreline. I could see that two people had already managed to swim to shore on their own and were huddled together, close to the water's edge. Three other victims were still trying to swim in on their own. It looked like the lifeguards weren't finished quite yet.

"Colleen and Andrea, please go check on the two sitting on the shoreline," Dillon said, pointing to the man and woman I had just spotted. "Sadie and Ted, why don't you check on the two the guards just pulled out of the water? Buddy and I will take care of the three who are swimming in now."

Colleen and I trekked over to the pair sitting on the beach. A young man and woman who looked to be in their early twenties looked up as we approached. Blood trickled from a gash on the man's deeply tanned right lower leg. Both appeared very fit, which I supposed explained how they managed to swim to safety on their own.

"How are you guys doing?" Colleen asked, as we knelt down next to them. "What are your names?"

"I'm Tyler, and this is Darlene. We're basically okay, but we're really worried about our friends. Do you think they'll be okay?"

"I think the guards will have everyone out within a few minutes," I replied, glancing back toward the water. "It looks like you have a pretty good cut on your leg. Does anything else hurt?"

"Yeah, I think I might need some stitches," Tyler responded. "This was supposed to be a really fun day. We decided to take a cruise for my birthday, but everything started going all wrong. The waves got too big for our boat to handle. We got pushed into the jetty."

"I'm so sorry to hear that," Colleen said. "The lifeguards are rescuing your friends right now. They're going to be okay."

"Do you really think they'll be all right?" Darlene asked. "One of them is my sister."

"It looks like the lifeguards are helping in the last couple of the swimmers now. We have several of our members waiting to help your sister as soon as she gets out of the water," Colleen replied.

I could see that Tyler and Darlene were both shivering hard. We quickly placed blankets around their shoulders. *We're going to need to get them out of the cold quickly.* I was concerned that they were entering the early stages of hypothermia.

Colleen carefully rinsed sand out of Tyler's leg wound, and I placed a sterile dressing over it. "Do you think you'll be able to walk on it?" I asked.

"I think I'll be fine," he answered. "I might need a hand, but I can walk."

"They're all out of the water!" Officer McGovern shouted.

"Thank God," Darlene murmured, hearing the lifeguard as well. "Praise God everyone's okay."

"We need to get you into the ambulance, where it's warmer," Colleen said. Arm in arm, bracing ourselves against the howling wind, we slowly walked toward our rigs.

Colleen and I loaded Darlene and Tyler into one of the ambulances and transported them to Bakersville Hospital. They both needed to be treated for cold exposure, and Tyler was also going to need stitches for the nasty gash on his leg. Dillon, Buddy, and the rest of the squad members transported the remaining victims to our first aid building to warm up and to make arrangements for transportation home.

A few hours later, I finally sat down with my bowl of Manhattan clam chowder. I was just finishing it up when my pager went off again.

DISPATCHER: "Request for first aid to stand by at the Wesley Avenue Beach for a ship being pulled up out of the ocean."

"You have to go back there *again?*" my father asked. "You just came home."

"Hopefully it won't take too long," I answered. I had no idea how long it would take to tow a boat out of the ocean. But at least this time,

I was better prepared with sweatpants, a hoodie, and a warm fleece-lined windbreaker.

The same crew of first aid members reassembled at the first aid building. This time, we brought two ambulances back to the scene. We parked alongside several of our town's fire trucks.

I noted that the boat had shifted its position over the past several hours. Instead of smashing against the jetty, it now was half-submerged closer to the shoreline.

"Sorry to bring you all back so soon, but the boat's a hazard to swimmers the way it is," Sergeant Flint explained. "Since it's heavily damaged and firmly stuck in the sand, it can't be towed out to sea and back to the marina. We're going to have to tow it up onto the beach instead."

"Since it's such an unusual procedure, we wanted the first aid squad here in case someone gets hurt," Officer McGovern added.

"This is going to take forever," Buddy sighed. "I'm going to wait in the rig for a bit to keep warm."

"Yeah, we're probably going to be here for a long time," Ted agreed. "I'll sit in the rig with you. Just call us if you need us to come back out."

The wind had picked up even more and the sand was blowing, which impaired visibility. A boat towing service had already attached the boat to a winch. We loaned our ropes to the fire department, and they tied them onto the boat for extra support. Fire department members, together with Sergeant Flint and Officer McGovern, heaved on the ropes with all their might.

For a while, it seemed as though the boat would never budge. "It looks like the winch is really struggling," Dillon said.

"We should help them," Colleen suggested. "If we do, maybe we'll get out of here sooner," she added.

"Sounds good to me," Sadie said, "though I'm not sure how much of a help I'll be." Sadie had a bright, cheerful personality which made answering calls together fun.

"Me too," I laughed. "But I guess every bit helps."

And so we joined together with the police and fire department to pull the ropes. Ever so slowly, inch by inch, the boat began to creep closer to shore. *We're doing it!*

Eventually, we successfully pulled the remnants of the boat up onto the shore. Tugging on a heavy boat entrenched in sand and half-covered with cold water was not exactly my idea of a good time, but there was definitely a feeling of satisfaction when we got the job done.

Within a few hours, I was back home and cozy in my own bed. It was truly fortunate that everyone was rescued that day. The boat was a total loss, but material possessions can be replaced. Lives cannot.

The Nursing Home Strikes Again

Stand up in the presence of the aged, show respect
for the elderly and revere your God. I am the LORD.
LEVITICUS 19:32

Amelia Baumgartner woke up and sat on the edge of her bed. *I'm hungry. If I could just find the kitchen in this place, maybe I could get a snack.*

Amelia, now 91 years old, knew that she was a little confused at times. That's why her daughter made her move into this place. Her daughter claimed it wasn't safe for Amelia to live on her own anymore. Amelia disagreed, but she finally gave in to her daughter's wishes. Now, she found herself vehemently wishing that she hadn't. She didn't care for this nursing home one bit.

She put on her slippers and padded slowly down the hallway. She hadn't eaten much at dinner because it looked and smelled terrible. *Some warm milk and graham crackers sure would hit the spot. Just like I always used to have when I was at home.* Amelia swallowed hard. She tried her best not to think about home anymore. It was too painful. Her home was gone now...sold. Now she had nothing except this horrible place.

Amelia spotted a door off to the right. *I bet that's the kitchen.* She turned the handle and stepped through the doorway. Amelia recognized her error almost immediately. She wasn't in the kitchen at all...she was outside, on a metal fire escape. She quickly tried to turn the door handle to go back inside, but it was too late. The door was now locked. *Now what am I going to do?* Amelia knocked on the door, hoping someone might hear her. "Hello! Let me back in!" she called. But no one responded.

It's so cold out here! I wish I had worn my robe. She shivered in her thin nylon nightgown. Amelia stepped back, and her foot slipped on a patch of ice. Losing her balance, she rolled over and over again down the entire flight of stairs. Just when she thought the tumbling would never end, she landed with a hard bang at the bottom.

Amelia got onto her hands and knees and tried to stand up, but couldn't. *My legs just won't cooperate anymore.* Amelia knew it was pointless to crawl back up the stairs and try banging on that door again. She figured no one would hear her anyway. *I'll just crawl over to one of the doors down there and knock. If I can find one, that is. I wish I could find my slippers. They must have fallen off somewhere on the stairs. It's so terribly dark out here. I can't see a thing.*

Amelia crawled for what seemed like an eternity to her, but she couldn't find a door. *I'm so very cold. I'm going to have to take a rest. I just can't go on anymore.* She collapsed down onto the frozen ground and closed her eyes. And prayed that someone would eventually find her.

. . . .

DISPATCHER: "Request for first aid at the nursing home for a fall victim."

I squelched a groan. Calls at the nursing home were frequent, and often not all that pleasant. Since it was a cold November night, I grabbed my heavy winter coat. We rolled the rig with Dillon, Ted, and me.

DISPATCHER: "Update: The call is outside, behind the building."

Outside, at two o'clock in the morning? What in the world was one of the residents doing out in the cold in the middle of the night? Or was the call for an employee? Now I was doubly glad I had worn my heavy coat. We grabbed our first aid kit and a flashlight and trekked around the building to where we could make out the dim outline of two police officers.

When I knelt down beside Sergeant Flint and Officer McGovern, I saw one of the most heart-wrenching figures I have ever laid my eyes on. A tiny, elderly woman, Amelia Baumgartner, lay unconscious on the cold ground, wearing only a thin short-sleeved nightgown. Deathly pale feet with blue toenails peeked out from the bottom of her gown. I could see that she had some nasty cuts and abrasions on her face, hands, arms, and feet. There was a large purplish bump on her forehead, framed by her wispy snow-white hair.

"How long has she been out here?" I asked, horrified. Her skin felt icy cold to the touch.

"Last seen by staff two hours ago," Officer McGovern answered. "It appears Mrs. Baumgartner went out an emergency exit and fell down the fire escape."

I looked more closely at the building. The fire escape was made out of metal; it was harsh, cold and unforgiving. There were easily twenty steps from the second floor. It seemed likely that she tumbled down the stairs and then crawled another thirty feet to where she now lay.

"Doesn't this place have alarms on the doors? Why didn't they find her sooner?" Dillon asked.

"Believe me, we're going to look into that. I suppose there may have been some sort of malfunction," Sergeant Flint replied.

Mrs. Baumgartner was extremely frail. She probably weighed no more than 90 pounds soaking wet. Unfortunately, she looked soaking wet. The ground must have still been wet from an earlier rain shower.

"No radial pulse, but I have a faint carotid," Dillon said. He couldn't obtain a blood pressure. Since he couldn't feel her radial pulse, we realized that Amelia's systolic blood pressure must be less than 80. That was too low. Dangerously low.

The medics arrived just as we were about to transfer Mrs. Baumgartner onto our backboard. We quickly caught Baxter and Roberta up to speed as to what had transpired thus far.

"She appears to have severe hypothermia with peripheral shutdown," Baxter said after a brief assessment. "We have to be very, very careful moving her onto this backboard. If we so much as even slightly bounce her, we may stop her heart instantly." He went on to explain that her heart was in an extremely precarious state. "There's a really good chance we are not going to get this woman to the hospital alive. As soon as we get her into the rig, get the ambu bag ready."

"Okay everybody, pretend she's like a really fine piece of china," Dillon said as we carefully moved Mrs. Baumgartner onto our backboard.

Four of us carried the backboard across the dark yard to our stretcher, which was parked near the ambulance. I took great care not to trip, realizing that a loss of footing could spell disaster for Mrs. Baumgartner. Baxter kept a close eye on the heart monitor as we walked. He was concerned that our footsteps could jar Mrs. Baumgartner's heart rhythm, potentially sending her into a fatal cardiac arrhythmia.

In the rig, we administered warmed, humidified oxygen via a nonrebreather mask. Ted placed a special hypothermia blanket on Mrs. Baumgartner, and I put a bunch of regular blankets on top of that to begin the warming process. Mrs. Baumgartner stirred but remained unconscious.

Because of the patient's hypothermia and peripheral shutdown, it was difficult for Baxter to gain IV access. After a few tries, however, he was successful, and I breathed a sigh of relief. At least now Mrs. Baumgartner could have access to potentially life-saving drugs. The warm saline solution dripped slowly into her vein. I hoped that each drop would improve her blood pressure and assist in raising her core temperature.

"She's still touch-and-go," Baxter said as we pulled up to the emergency room. By now, we knew the routine. We lifted the stretcher out with extreme care, placing it very gently on the concrete behind the ambulance.

I silently fumed over the injustice of it all. One of our most vulnerable citizens, a woman who was supposed to be under 24-hour care, lay near death on the icy cold ground for close to two hours. This woman was someone's mother, someone's grandmother. Someone had paid a lot of money to ensure her care and safety. The system had failed her.

We learned that after several weeks in the intensive care unit, Mrs. Baumgartner finally became well enough to be discharged. I heard that her family sent her to a different nursing home.

. . . .

DISPATCHER: "Request for first aid at the nursing home for a choking victim."

It was two o'clock in the morning, and only three of us responded to the call: Jose, Ted, and me. "It's a choking victim, so I guess we should be okay with just the three of us," Ted said. Oftentimes with choking calls, the person coughs up the object before we even get there. We rarely have to transport the patient to the hospital.

"Okay then, let's roll. We probably aren't going to get anyone else anyway," I replied. *Hopefully, this will be a nice, quick call and I can go right back to bed.* However, before our rig even left our building, our pagers went off again.

DISPATCHER: "Update: CPR is in progress."

"Yikes," Jose said. "It sounds like our choking victim just took a turn for the worse."

"Now I really wish we had more members," I lamented. Performing CPR with only three people is not a picnic.

"Please tap the call out again for additional manpower to meet us at the scene," Jose said to the dispatcher. The dispatcher did so, but no one else responded. That's just the way it goes sometimes.

We piled the first aid kit, oxygen, suction unit, and defibrillator on top of the stretcher and hustled through a bunch of narrow halls and then into the elevator. The patient's room was just a few doors down from the elevator on the second floor.

As I entered the room, the first thing I noticed was that it reeked of peanut butter. Sergeant Flint and Officer McGovern were performing CPR on an elderly man. Or, I should say, they were trying to perform CPR.

"Can't get an airway," Officer Flint said, shaking his head in frustration.

"Chunky peanut butter," Officer McGovern added, nodding his head toward a jar on the floor.

I wanted to say "Yuck," but managed to keep the thought to myself.

"Milton is 94. History is significant for Alzheimer's. That's all we've got," Officer Flint said, scooping a chunk of peanut butter from Milton's mouth.

The officers moved out of the way, happy to let us take over. I moistened the suction unit and started sucking peanut butter out of Milton's mouth. But it kept coming and coming and coming.

"Tell the dispatcher to tap it out again," Ted directed Officer Flint. "We need more help."

Dispatcher Franklin tapped out a third request, but as fate would have it, no other members responded. We continued with our efforts. Jose tried to get some breaths in with the ambu bag, but the air just wouldn't go in. It seemed as though Milton's whole airway was clogged with chunky peanut butter. *This poor, poor man. This is absolutely horrible!*

I glanced at the peanut butter container. A stainless steel spoon stuck out crookedly from the top of the container, which was half-empty. I wasn't sure how full it was when Milton started his late-night peanut butter eating spree, but I guessed that it must have been pretty close to full. I kept suctioning. More peanut butter came out. And

more. And more. And more. It was so thick, it kept clogging the suction catheter. I ran more water through the line and proceeded to suck
out more peanut butter. "It just keeps coming and coming," I said. If
we didn't clear his airway soon, Milton would have virtually no chance
at resuscitation.

Jose pressed the analyze button on the defibrillator, which indicated
that Milton was still in a non-shockable rhythm. "We're going to need
to get him on a backboard," he said.

We rolled Milton onto a backboard just as the medics, Ty and Paula,
arrived. As Ted explained what was going on, I kept suctioning out
more peanut butter. And more. And more. "If this keeps up, I'm going
to have to change the suction chamber," I murmured. "I'm not sure
how much more peanut butter can fit in here."

One of the medics hooked him up to a heart monitor. "Stop CPR,"
Paula said. After analyzing the rhythm, she said, "He's in asystole. You
can keep going with the chest compressions now."

Ty prepared for intubation. He opened Milton's mouth and tried
to insert the laryngoscope. "We're going to need to get rid of this peanut butter before I can do anything," he said.

I pointed to the suction unit. "Maybe you can give it a try. I've
already suctioned out a ton…it seems almost futile." *Lord, I hope Milton didn't suffer much before he went unconscious.*

"Are you kidding? All that came out of him? How long has the call
been going on at this point?" Ty asked.

"About 25 minutes since dispatch," Jose answered.

Ty shook his head. "The patient's cool to the touch now and is getting stiff. There's no way I'm going to be able to intubate him with all
this peanut butter. I'm calling this in to the doc," he said.

A few short minutes later, Milton was officially pronounced dead
by the paramedics. I couldn't help but think that is was not a very
nice way to exit this world. It must have been so frightening for him,
unable to get any air into his lungs. By the time staff found him, he
was already pulseless. He died alone, on the floor, unable to breathe
because of peanut butter. In my opinion, Milton should not have been

left unattended with the container of chunky peanut butter in the first place. I felt like it was a preventable death.

I was struck by the similarity to the first aid call for Amelia. Milton's care had been entrusted to others, but the system failed him. I reflected that sometimes, the elderly are some of the most vulnerable of God's children.

The Train Tragedy

*Then he said to them, "My soul is overwhelmed with sorrow
to the point of death. Stay here and keep watch with me."*

MATTHEW 26:38

Matthew Reed looked at his two friends, Marta Jacobs and Donna Bradley, and couldn't help but grin. *What a fun night!* It felt great to be with his high school buddies again. He loved college, but it was hard work. *It's so nice to be able to relax, forget about studying, and just enjoy watching game three of the World Series.* "I wish this night would never end," he said wistfully, almost to himself. At this moment, life was perfect.

"That's ridiculous," Marta laughed. "Then we would never get to see game four."

The people in the restaurant broke into a rousing cheer as one of the teams scored another run. "I'm with you, Matthew. Life doesn't get any better than this," Donna said.

The three friends continued to laugh and chat until the game was over. Donna glanced at her watch. "I should probably be getting home, guys. I've got to get up early tomorrow for work."

"Yeah, I hear you," Matthew said. "I've got to get up early tomorrow too. My sister Suzie has a big basketball game up north and I want to see how she does." Matthew had played basketball with his sister since childhood. He liked to think she was such an amazing player partly due to his guidance.

The trio paid their dinner bill and headed out to the parking lot.

"Maybe we can do this again tomorrow night for game four. What do you think?" Marta asked.

"Count me in," Matthew said. "Let's pick a different place, though, for some variety."

"I'm in too," Donna said. "After tomorrow, I'm off work for two days."

The three slid into Matthew's small sedan and pulled out onto the highway. "Can you drop me off first?" Donna asked. "I really need to get some sleep, dudes."

"No problem, I gotcha covered," Matthew said. "I'm really tired too. Way too much studying." A few minutes later, Matthew pulled up in front of Donna's house on Kingston Avenue. "Goodnight. I'll see you tomorrow, maybe around 7:30, okay?"

"Sounds good. Goodnight, guys," Donna replied.

"Night."

Matthew pulled away and stopped at the railroad crossing. The gates were down. *Why are the gates always down? It seems like every time I try to cross the tracks, the gates are down. How is that even possible?*

Matthew and Marta waited for several minutes. "Where in the world is the train? It's taking forever," Marta said. She rolled her window down. "I can't even hear the train's engine."

"Maybe the gates are broken," Matthew suggested. Slowly, he crept closer to the gates and hung his head out the window. "I don't see anything coming on my side. Do you?" he asked.

. . . .

DISPATCHER: "Request for first aid at Kingston Avenue and the railroad tracks for a car hit by a train."

As I hurriedly got ready to go, I flipped on my police scanner just in time to hear Sergeant Flint say, "There are two bodies." I noticed that he used the word *bodies* and not *patients*. That didn't sound promising.

I could feel my heart pounding in my chest as I drove straight to the scene; I wasn't sure what to expect. It was very dark on the tracks and I squinted to get my bearings. Officer Sims pointed his flashlight off into the distance. "One of your patients is over there," he said to me.

I ran along the tracks, careful not to trip on the big stones. I wasn't sure, but I thought I heard someone say the word *DOA*. DOA stands for "dead on arrival." *I really hope I heard wrong.*

I found Gary kneeling down at a young man's head. The victim looked like he was only two or three years younger than me. "I'm holding stabilization," he said. "He's going to need an ambu bag and fast."

"I thought I heard someone say he was a DOA," I managed to say. The poor young man certainly looked like he could have been a DOA, except that I could see that his chest was still rising and falling. Amazingly, he was still breathing. *Please, Lord, we need Your help.*

"I got a weak carotid pulse of 68," Gary said. "But I'm not sure how long it's going to last. His respiratory rate is 40."

One of our young probationary members, Flynn Adams, ran up with the first aid kit and a flashlight. I pulled out the ambu bag and tried as best as I could to fit the mask to the victim's face and started giving rescue breaths. I couldn't insert an oral airway because of the facial trauma, and I couldn't insert a nasopharyngeal airway because of the possibility of brain trauma. *We'll just have to do without until the medics can intubate him.*

Flynn directed the flashlight onto the patient's face. "I heard Officer Sims say that his name is Matthew. He's twenty-one years old," he said simply. I glanced up at him to make sure he was okay. Matthew was a mere three years older than Flynn.

I brushed a strand of long blond hair off the victim's face and gently wiped some blood that was flowing from the corner of his mouth. I was grateful for the light, but at the same time worried that Flynn was witnessing something so upsetting. "I'm going to need the suction for this blood," I said. "Would you mind running for it?"

"No problem," Flynn said, disappearing into the dark. A minute later, the fire department illuminated the scene with large floodlights.

Now I could see that Mason, Chris, and several of our other members were huddled across the tracks underneath an old hickory tree.

Gary caught the direction of my gaze. "That patient's name is Marta. She's definitely a DOA," he said. "I checked in over there first to see what they needed and the police sent me over here."

My heart squeezed painfully at this news, but I knew I had to shake it off and not dwell on it. *Focus on Matthew and don't think about how incredibly horrible this whole situation is.* My gaze briefly fell on what I thought was a pile of twisted scrap metal near Matthew. With surprise, I suddenly realized it was actually a large chunk of what used to be his car. Another large chunk lay close to Marta. Later, I learned that the car literally split in two upon impact with the train.

"Let's get him on a backboard," Gary said. "Maybe we can get him packaged up before the medics arrive." Flynn clicked the last strap into place just as Baxter and Roberta arrived from the hospital. Baxter came over to check on Matthew, while Roberta went to Marta.

"What's the story?" Baxter asked as he began preparing to intubate the patient.

"Well, it appears that their car was hit by a train," Gary replied. He filled Baxter in on the details of our assessment.

Roberta joined us a few minutes later. "I'm afraid there's not much we can do for the girl…she's going to end up being a pronouncement. Let me get an IV going for you."

"Thanks," Baxter said. "And please check lung sounds for me; I think the tube placement is good."

Officer Sims checked in with us during his scene investigation. "How's he doing? Are you taking him to Bakersville?"

"Well, he's still alive," Gary replied. "We'll be taking him to Bakersville in a couple of minutes."

"Tell the ER staff I'll be up there a little later," Officer Sims said. *It's going to be a long night for the men in blue.*

We hustled Matthew into the back of our ambulance. The rig was packed: Roberta, Baxter, Gary, and I squeezed in. Buddy drove our rig and Helen drove the medics' rig.

"We need to try to keep him stable," Baxter said. "Keep up with that suction."

During the course of the trip, Gary and I suctioned at least a half-bottle of blood from Matthew's mouth. I wasn't sure if the blood was only coming from Matthew's oral injuries or if it was coming up from his stomach too. He had bruising around his eyes and some fluid leaking from his ears, telling us that he potentially had a significant head injury.

"He's probably got massive internal bleeding," Baxter said, keeping an eye on the heart monitor. "They're going to have to rush him into surgery if he's going to have a chance." Matthew's pressure was dangerously low, and he was at high risk for going into shock.

We all knew the situation was grim. But we were doing everything in our power to help Matthew. Bakersville Hospital's trauma team met us at the emergency room doors. "Follow me," one of the nurses said, and led us straight into a trauma bay. After we transferred over patient care, I took one long last look at Matthew. *It's hard to be so involved and then to suddenly have to just let go.* I quietly slipped out of the room. Gary, who was assisting with the ambu bag, stayed behind to help.

Gary came out of the room about ten minutes later, looking decidedly pale. "They cracked his chest open right in front of my eyes...I've never seen anything like that before," he said. "They're taking him straight to the OR."

"You guys did a great job," Baxter said. "You got him here alive."

Baxter meant well, but his words didn't make me feel much better. I didn't have much hope that Matthew would pull through, and if he did, I was afraid his quality of life would be very poor. I glanced at my watch. *2:15 a.m. I can't believe it's already 2:15 in the morning.*

"We'll head back to the scene and see if they need anything else from us," Buddy said.

When we arrived back on Kingston Avenue, I studied the scene more closely. Matthew's college cap lay on the ground near an evergreen bush and his music CDs lay scattered close by. *Will he ever get a chance to listen to his favorite tunes again?*

Officer Sims signaled us to come over to Marta. A sheet lay over her. "I need to get her in your rig. I'm concerned that bystanders may try to get a look at her," Officer Sims said. "The coroner should be here within a half hour and then we'll just transfer her to his vehicle."

With a heavy heart, I helped to roll Marta onto a backboard and place her in our ambulance. I was glad she was covered with the sheet; I didn't really want to see her face. It would make it more real, more heartbreaking, more haunting.

The coroner, Jackson Zane, arrived as predicted a half hour later. He was an odd-looking fellow with long brown hair but a shiny bald dome. He always wore circa 1960s glasses and checkered pants. With heavy hearts, we transferred Marta from our backboard to the coroner's gurney.

"Listen up, everybody," Officer Sims called out. "I need all of you to grab a flashlight and start looking. Word is that we may have a third victim here somewhere."

Helen let out a gasp of surprise. "Did you just say we may have a third victim?"

"Yes, we just got word that there may have been a third person in the car, by the name of Donna Bradley. She lives just a couple houses down from here. We've contacted her parents. They said she never made it home."

I was shocked. It was now one and a half hours past the initial dispatch. *A third victim?!* If the third victim's chances were slim before, they would be practically nonexistent now. The thought of a young woman lying injured and alone somewhere out here in the dark was almost too dreadful to contemplate. *I really, really wish we had known sooner.* As I grabbed a flashlight, I fought down a wave of nausea.

For twenty long minutes, we painstakingly searched for Donna Bradley. *Dear Lord, please let us find this young woman soon.*

But as much as I hoped we would find Donna soon, at the same time I felt almost afraid to find her…afraid that she would be dead…afraid of what she might look like. I felt consumed with guilt. We should have started looking for her sooner. But we just didn't know.

"Call off the search," Officer Sims said. Word quickly spread down the chain of EMS and fire volunteers. "We've got her."

"Does she need first aid?" Buddy asked.

"No, she's fine," Officer Sims replied. "She's home with her parents now. Apparently, she witnessed the accident from her front porch. She was so overcome that she...ran away."

What a terrible burden for that young woman to live with for the rest of her life. But thank God, at least she lived. Apparently, Donna saw her friends' car come to a full stop in front of the railroad gates. But then, she heard the impact, witnessed the devastation, and tried to get away from the horror of it all.

"We're done with our investigation. If you don't mind, could you please help us to pick up the pieces of car? Once word gets out, a lot of people will be streaming over here later in the morning to try to get a look," Officer Sims said.

As I bent over to pick up car scraps, I thought of Marta's and Matthew's parents. Marta's parents must be absolutely devastated, trying to come to grips with the fact that their beloved daughter was gone. Matthew's parents were probably in the OR waiting room, praying for a miracle. *Please be with them, Lord.*

When we were just about done, Helen gave me a hug. "I just heard news about Matthew," she said.

"And?" I prompted.

She shook her head. "He didn't make it. He died during surgery."

I wasn't surprised that Matthew didn't make it, but I had been hoping against hope that it would turn out okay. But it was not to be. "It's so sad...so incredibly sad," I said. No words seemed adequate to describe the tragedy.

"We're going to call for the critical incident stress debriefing team to meet with us tonight," Helen said. "I think we could all use some counseling to help us through this."

"Good idea. I'd like to hear what they have to say," I said. I had heard about the critical incident stress debriefing team during my continuing education courses, but I had never been to an actual debriefing. The team includes a group of volunteers trained to assist EMS after particularly disturbing calls. I knew we needed them. I was worried about the effect of the call not only on our youngest and newest members, but on our veteran members as well.

I got home at 5:00 a.m. *Only one hour until I have to get up for work. It's pointless to even try going back to bed.* I felt tired, but my mind was racing. Feeling almost numb, I took a shower and went through the motions of getting ready for work. To make it even worse, as soon as I arrived at work, I had to give my coworkers a lecture about osteoporosis.

Before I knew it, it was time to speak in front of my department. I felt pasty and shaky. *How am I ever going to make it through the lecture?* I knew I was very distracted; my mind kept going back to the accident scene. I thought of poor Matthew and Marta. And then I tried not to think about them. *Is my lecture even making any sense? Please just let me finish this soon.*

I finally made it through the lecture. Barely. And I dragged myself through the rest of the workday. I knew I had to stay busy. Because if I didn't, I knew I would see Matthew's face. When I got home, I found out that the squad would be meeting with the debriefing team in three hours.

"Do you have to go?" my mom asked. "You didn't get any sleep last night. Maybe you should go straight to bed." I knew she was worried. I appreciated her love and support.

"Mom, I really need to go. I think it will help me to fall asleep better tonight. I'm afraid that when I go to bed, I'll think about the accident…"

Mom gave me a hug. "Well then, it sounds like you better go. I hope they have some good advice for all of you."

And so our squad and community members pulled together to begin the difficult healing process.

………………

Several days after the debriefing, several of us chatted for a few minutes outside of our first aid building.

"I thought the debriefing team was excellent," Helen said.

"Yes, it was really great for everyone to have a chance to share their feelings," I replied.

By law, the trains blow their whistles at each intersection as they travel through our town. I noticed that for the next several weeks after the accident, the whistle seemed magnified somehow. A noise that normally was just part of the background was now in the forefront of my consciousness. Many other members who responded to the train call reported experiencing the same phenomena.

Time passed and eventually the whistle once again faded into background noise. A memorial marks the spot where Matthew and Marta so tragically lost their lives. Although their lives on earth were cut short, I took comfort in the fact that they were now with the Lord. *Dear Lord, please bring comfort to Matthew and Marta's families.*

Fire!

*You, LORD, keep my lamp burning; my
God turns my darkness into light.*

PSALM 18:28

I have the utmost respect for firefighters. While most people want to run out of a burning building, firefighters are running in. Our fire department spends countless hours training and drilling so they will be prepared, no matter what they face.

One evening, our squad drilled together with the fire department at a home that was scheduled to be torn down the next morning. The homeowner had agreed to let the house be utilized to simulate a fire situation. This allows for more realistic training for the department.

I watched from the sidelines as the fire department pumped the house full of artificial smoke. Our squad was mainly there to stand by and support the firefighters, just in case something went wrong. If one of the firefighters overheated or needed oxygen, we would be close by to assist.

"How would you like to come inside and drill with us?" Ray Watson, the fire chief, invited us. Ray was a friendly fellow with a warm smile. He had been a member of our first aid squad for several years, but eventually gave it up due to the time commitment of being on both the fire department and the first aid squad. "You can see what it's like to wear a Scott air pack." A Scott pack is a self-contained breathing apparatus that provides a firefighter with breathable air during a fire or smoke condition. "We also have mannequins on the second floor,"

Ray continued. "You can try carrying one out if you like. I'm going in myself for a bit, so you could even follow me."

Gary and I exchanged looks. It sounded intriguing to me. I thought it would be interesting to see what firefighters experience, but without the pressure of a real-life situation. It took us less than a second to take him up on his offer. "We're in," we said in unison.

A couple of firemen helped us get on the turnout gear and Scott packs. The gear seemed cumbersome and the pack felt heavy. Gary and I slowly followed Ray up a flight of stairs. I kept one hand on the wall and tried not to lose my balance. I was actually familiar with the house because I used to pet-sit for the owner's dog. The home had always been bright and sunny, but now it seemed dark and foreboding. Since it was so smoky, I couldn't see more than a foot or two in front of me. *I am so glad this is not a real fire!*

"Are you okay?" Gary called back to me.

I grunted a non-committal reply. I wasn't sure how I was. I would be glad once this was over. I stayed as close to Gary as I could. I definitely did not want to get lost!

"Here's your victim," Ray said, pointing off to the left. I squinted and could barely make out the outline of a figure on the floor. I supposed it was one of the mannequins Ray had mentioned.

"Why don't you go ahead and try first," Gary suggested, motioning with his hand since it was difficult to hear.

"Okay, I'll give it a try," I replied. I attempted to pick the mannequin up, but it was too heavy for me. I tried to drag it, but it was extremely difficult. I felt awkward with all the turnout gear on, and I couldn't even get a good handle on the mannequin. Eventually, Gary gave me a hand and together we dragged the dummy toward the stairs.

Even though I was young and fairly strong, I was really only capable of looking out for myself in that simulated fire situation. And I knew beyond a shadow of a doubt that I would never want to be in a real fire situation. The drill was plenty real enough for me, and it renewed my appreciation of our firefighters.

....

Chet Chamberlin woke from a deep sleep to a piercing, ear-splitting noise. *What in the world is that?* Groggily, he rolled over and sat up on the edge of the bed. Suddenly recognizing the sound, Chet sprang bolt upright in bed. It was his fire alarm!

The acrid smell of smoke filled his nose and he heard an odd crackling noise. *Dear God, please tell me that's not a fire making that noise.*

Almost in disbelief, he stood up and walked over to his bedroom door. He placed a hand on it and decided it felt warm, but not hot. He quickly grabbed a towel from his bathroom, moistened it with water and placed it over his mouth, and then stepped out into the hallway.

"Tabitha! Tabitha! We need to go outside!" he cried out. He and his wife, Dorothy, had adopted Tabitha when she was just a kitten. Now Dorothy was gone and Tabitha was pushing 15. He loved that cat to pieces; she was what gave him a reason to get out of bed each morning. *I have to find her!*

The smoke burned Chet's eyes. He grabbed the railing and carefully made his way downstairs. Tabitha often liked to sleep curled up behind the sofa. Slowly, he made his way through the smoke toward the living room. "Tabitha!" he called again. It was impossible to see anything. *Where is she?*

Flames started to creep up behind him in their race to consume his home. It was getting harder and harder to breathe, and he felt like the heat was starting to sear his lungs. *If I don't get out now, I'll probably never get out. But I don't want to leave without Tabitha.* He called for her once more, and then knew that it was no use. Shoulders slumping in defeat, Chet staggered out the front door and onto his lawn.

....

DISPATCHER: "Request for fire and first aid at 82 Sunset Drive for a working structure fire."

It was just three days before Christmas. I'm not sure why, but many of our worst fire calls seem like they occur around the holidays. Sadie, Dillon, Ted, and I responded with the ambulance to the scene.

We parked down the road from the fire to keep out of the way of the fire trucks. As I looked out the window of the ambulance, my heart sank at the sight. The home, a modest two-story structure, was fully engulfed in bright orange flames. It looked like it was going to be a total loss. *Every family photo, every Christmas ornament, every knick-knack, each and every stick of furniture...will all be gone. Some Christmas this family is going to have.* I sighed, struck by the sadness of it all.

"Wow, it's really cooking," Sadie whistled. "I hope everyone got out okay."

The Fire Chief, Ray Watson, called us on the radio. "We have one patient for you with smoke inhalation. He's on the neighbor's front porch right now."

The four of us grabbed our necessary equipment and walked quickly down the street. We found an older gentleman hunched over in a wicker chair, his back turned toward his home. "I just can't bear to look," I heard him say to his neighbor.

Officer Sims was standing next to the two men. "This is Chet Chamberlin, age 77," he said. "I think he may have taken in quite a bit of smoke before he managed to get out."

"Sir, we're going to walk you over to the ambulance and have you sit in the back, where it's warmer. We'll give you some oxygen and hopefully that will help you feel a little better," Dillon said.

Dillon and Ted each placed an arm around Chet and led him toward our ambulance. Chet looked utterly deflated. All of his worldly possessions were going up in smoke...literally. *It must be one of the worst feelings in the world. Please comfort him, Lord.*

We helped Chet to lie down on our cot, but first we elevated the head of the stretcher to make it easier for Chet to breathe. "How are you doing, Mr. Chamberlin?" Ted asked.

"My lungs are burning," Chet said. "I stayed inside, looking for my cat, Tabitha..."

I could tell from the way he left the sentence hanging that he must not have found his cat. "I'm so sorry," I said.

Chet nodded, and his eyes became teary. "Thank you." He cleared his throat and picked an imaginary piece of lint off his trousers.

Dillon put an oxygen mask on Mr. Chamberlin while I took a set of vital signs. Blood pressure, pulse, and respiratory rate were all okay. *But I don't think his broken heart is okay.*

"I couldn't find Tabitha," he said. "She's almost 15 years old. My wife Dorothy, God rest her soul, passed away last year...She loved that cat."

Losing his wife last year sounded like it had been the first blow. Now his house was burning to the ground, and it appeared as though Tabitha had expired in the fire as well. I wished there was something I could do to ease some of Mr. Chamberlin's pain.

"We want to take you up to the hospital to get checked out," Dillon said. "You took in a lot of smoke."

"I don't know. I kind of want to stay here and see how it goes. I'm actually feeling a little bit better now, with the oxygen. Really, I'm okay. I'm going to call my son, and if I don't feel well later, he can take me to the emergency room."

I was glad to hear that Mr. Chamberlin had a son. At least he had somewhere to go and wasn't totally alone. I could appreciate that it would be very difficult to leave with so much still going on at his house. The big flames were gone, but there was still quite a bit of smoke.

I listened to Mr. Chamberlin's lung sounds. They were clear, but I was still concerned about the smoke he had inhaled. "We can't force you to go, but we do recommend you go to the hospital and get looked at." Before I could finish my sentence, the rear door to the ambulance opened. Chief Watson stepped in, holding a tiny, soot-covered cat.

"Tabitha!" Chet cried out. "I don't believe it! Where did you find her?" *The answer to a prayer!*

Smiling, Chief Watson carefully placed Tabitha in Mr. Chamberlin's arms. "One of our men found her hiding in a downstairs closet."

Sadie grabbed a pediatric oxygen mask from the cabinet and carefully placed it in front of Tabitha's face. "How about some oxygen, little kitty?"

Tears of joy and gratitude filled Mr. Chamberlin's eyes. "How can I ever repay you?" he asked Ray.

Chief Watson smiled. "You just did," he said.

"Forget the hospital," Mr. Chamberlin said. "I need to get my baby to the vet."

It was truly a Christmas miracle. The fact that the fire department had rescued Tabitha was an extraordinary Christmas blessing. Most of Mr. Chamberlin's worldly possessions were probably gone, but at least now he would have his precious furry friend to help him through the difficult times ahead.

Keeping Up with Kids

God is our refuge and strength, an
ever-present help in trouble.

PSALM 46:1

Brendan, Meg, and I were at the first aid building cleaning up the rig when our pagers went off.

DISPATCHER: "Request for first aid at 1006 Crestview Drive for a seven-year-old girl with seizures."

"I'll drive," Brendan said. "Hop in."

I wondered if the child was having a febrile seizure or if she had a history of epilepsy. Seven seemed a bit old to me for a febrile seizure; we usually see that more in infants and younger children. I said a quick, silent prayer for our patient.

"House is on the right," Brendan said as we pulled up in front of a small brown ranch house. I grabbed the pediatric first aid kit while Meg picked up the clipboard and an oxygen tank.

"Nice swing," I said, pointing to an old-fashioned tire swing in the side yard.

"Doesn't sound like anyone will be using that today," Brendan replied, ringing the doorbell.

I heard footsteps, and then a woman swung the door open. "Thank goodness you're here," she said, nervously wringing her hands.

"Hannah's in her bedroom. Follow me, please." She led us through a living room with dark oak paneling to the rear of the home.

Hannah Hutchinson was a slim girl with long, glossy dark hair. She lay flat on her bed with her eyes closed, and her right arm stood straight up in the air. As a first aid squad member, I am more used to patients having full-body tonic-clonic type seizures. This was a new one for me.

Hannah's father, a short man with a stocky frame, sat next to his daughter on the edge of her bed. "I'm Nick Hutchinson and this is my wife, Lindsay, and daughter, Hannah," he said. "Thanks for coming. We think Hannah's having another seizure."

"I feel like it's my fault," Lindsay said, as tears began streaming down her face.

Nick stepped toward his wife and put his arm around her shoulders. "Honey, of course it's not your fault. You didn't make her have a seizure."

"No, but I scolded Hannah a few minutes ago and sent her to her room. When I came back to check on her, I found her like this. What have I done?" she asked.

"I'm sure scolding her wouldn't cause a seizure," Meg said, trying to calm Lindsay's fears. "Let's take a closer look at Hannah."

"She had a seizure like this once before," her father explained. "It was during a fever. It affected only one arm, just like it is now."

"How long ago was that?" I asked.

"Three years or so," Hannah's father said. "She was admitted to the hospital for two days."

I was perplexed; I had definitely never seen a seizure quite like this before. Hannah appeared unresponsive: She did not respond to voice and she did not react when Meg gently shook her shoulder. Her body remained very still and her right arm remained rigidly up in the air. While Meg took a set of vital signs, I gave Hannah oxygen. Even as I placed the mask by her face, she did not stir. My concern was growing and I was relieved when medics Ty and Paula arrived.

"How long has she been like this?" Paula asked, placing the back of her hand on Hannah's forehead to check her skin temperature.

"Going on fifteen minutes now," Nick replied. "The last time this happened, I think it only lasted about five minutes."

"Do you think she's going to be okay?" Lindsay asked. "I'll never forgive myself if she isn't." Her eyes began welling up with tears again.

Paula assessed Hannah carefully. "I have just one more thing to check," she said. The hand drop test is a test for unconsciousness. It's really pretty simple. The EMT or medic lifts up the patient's hand and very quickly lets it go directly over the face. If given only a split second to decide, the average person will not want to strike his own face. So, if the hand hits the face, that indicates the person is indeed unconscious. If the hand avoids the face, that points to the possibility that the patient is not truly unconscious.

Paula lifted Hannah's left (unaffected) arm over her face and let go. I held my breath, guessing her hand would plunk down on her nose. I was wrong! Hannah's left arm gracefully bypassed her face and landed gently on the bed. I was truly surprised. *How can a seven-year-old be that devious?* Apparently, Hannah was on her way to winning a Tony Award for best Broadway actress. Ty pulled Hannah's parents aside and quietly explained the significance of the test.

"Are you insinuating that Hannah may be faking? I absolutely refuse to believe that! She's having a seizure!" Nick exclaimed.

"I'm not saying definitively one way or the other," Ty said, trying to placate him. "I just wanted to make you aware of the possibility."

Lindsay, who had quietly absorbed the information from Ty, finally spoke up. "It's funny now that you mention it. A few weeks ago, Hannah asked me all kinds of questions about exactly what her seizure was like when she was younger. At first, I thought it was a coincidence that she should have another one so soon after asking me about it, but now I'm not so sure that it's a coincidence at all. Maybe she really is faking."

"Do you really think so?" Nick asked. He seemed to ponder the notion for a moment, and then slowly added, "Hannah's a very intelligent child. I suppose it's possible…"

Lindsay sat down on the bed next to her daughter. "Hannah, if you are doing this just to get attention, you need to stop, okay? We have the police and first aid here to help you. But if you don't really need help, we should let them leave so that they can go help someone who really does need help." Hannah did not respond to her mother's plea.

She kept her eyes firmly closed and her right arm remained straight up in the air.

"I think it's best if we take her to the hospital to get checked out," Paula said. "Better to err on the side of caution." We lifted Hannah onto our stretcher and placed her in the ambulance. During the ride to the hospital, Paula tried several times to gently bring Hannah's arm back down, but it stubbornly rose back up again.

While we brought Hannah into an emergency room cubicle, Paula and Ty reported their findings to Maggie, the triage nurse, as well as Dr. Morgan. Since we were curious about what they would find, Brendan, Meg, and I hung out for a few minutes by the triage desk.

It didn't take very long for the ER staff to confirm our suspicions. Eventually, caving in to pressure from Dr. Morgan and Maggie, Hannah came clean. "I was mad that I got sent to my room. I was getting back at my parents," she admitted.

If Hannah could pull off that kind of performance at age seven, I shudder to think what she would be capable of as a teenager. I wished her parents good luck.

....

"Please, please play hide-and-seek with me," four-year-old Jeffrey begged his grandmother, Lila Green. Lila, a kind and loving grandmother, doted on her grandson.

"You really should take a nap now, sweetheart," Lila said. "Your mom said to make sure you get a good nap."

"Hide-and-seek first," Jeffrey said stubbornly. "Nap later."

Maybe a quick game won't hurt. He'll keep asking me until I give in anyway. "Okay, little man. One game. That's it. Then it's naptime."

"Yay!" Jeffrey shouted excitedly. "I'll hide first!" With that, he scooted out of the kitchen. "Make sure you close your eyes!"

"Of course I will," Lila said. "I'll count to thirty. One-two-three…" *I'm so blessed to have Jeffrey in my life. He keeps me young.* "Twenty-nine, thirty. Ready or not, here I come!"

Lila and Jeffrey had played the game many times before. He had three favorite hiding spots: under the dining room table, in the bathtub, and behind the living room sofa. It usually took Lila all of two minutes to find him, but of course she pretended she didn't see him at first and kept "looking," much to her grandson's delight!

That's odd. He's not in any of his usual spots today. Lila searched room by room, calling Jeffrey's name. When she reached the last room and hadn't found him, she started to feel uneasy. *Where could that child be?* Lila started all over again, in the kitchen. "Please come out, Jeffrey. I don't want to play anymore. You win. I can't find you. It's naptime now."

The house was silent. Lila continued to recheck each room for any sign of Jeffrey. She glanced at her watch. Fifteen minutes had passed since they started this game. *Could he have slipped outside when I was upstairs looking for him? He's not dressed for the outdoors.* Lila shuddered at the thought. He wasn't even wearing a sweatshirt, and it was only about 40 degrees outside. She checked her front and backyard for Jeffrey, but with no success.

"Jeffrey, please come out! I really need you, sweetie! We can bake your favorite cookies if you come out now!"

Lila's offer was met with silence, and her level of concern escalated even further. She made one more frantic search of the house, urgently calling out her grandson's name. Panicking, she picked up the phone and dialed 911. "I'd like to report a missing child," she said, trying to control her mounting anxiety. *Please, God, help me to find Jeffrey!*

. . . .

DISPATCHER: "Request for manpower on Chestnut Street to assist in finding a missing child."

I was familiar with the street. My sister and I used to babysit for a girl who lived close to there. Barry, Colleen, Ted, and I climbed out of the ambulance to get instructions from Officer Endicott. "We're looking for a missing four-year-old boy named Jeffrey. He was playing hide-and-seek with his grandmother, but she couldn't find him. She searched the home and became concerned that he may have slipped outside. At that point, she called 911," he said.

"How long has he been missing?" Barry asked.

Officer Endicott glanced at his watch. "About forty-five minutes. We already searched inside. We decided to call you and the fire department to help us search outside, since it's a fairly large area to cover."

Every minute counts when a young child is missing. I recalled that there were numerous ponds and large sewer pipes nearby that could spell disaster for a four-year-old. Mentally, I didn't really want to go there yet. *Dear God, help us find this little guy quickly.*

"I want you to break into pairs. You two head north," Officer Endicott said, pointing to Ted and me. "And you two head west," he instructed Barry and Colleen.

Ted and I began searching the surrounding yards to the north. We took turns shouting, "Jeffrey!" *It's really cold outside and it's going to get dark soon. We need to find him quickly.* Ted and I approached a small pond. I searched for any sign of little Jeffrey and breathed a sigh of relief when there was none. *Please let us find him, but not in a pond!*

"All units, report back to base," I heard Officer Endicott say over our portable radios.

"Great, I hope they found him!" Ted said. "I remember I got lost once when I was little. Here I am seventy years later, and I still remember it like it was yesterday!"

"That must have been pretty traumatic. Well, let's hope they found him and he's okay," I said. We quickly made our way back to the Green residence.

"Good news, everybody. We found Jeffrey. We searched the house again, and he was inside after all," Officer Endicott said.

"Where was he?" Barry asked. "Garage? Under a bed?"

"Actually, he was sound asleep under a pile of clothes in the master bedroom closet. Apparently, Jeffrey is *very* good at hiding. When we searched the closet and called his name the first time, he didn't make a peep! I guess he was sleeping so soundly he didn't hear us."

Jeffrey was sitting at the kitchen table in his grandmother's lap. He still looked a bit sleepy and had lines on his face where he must have been lying on the clothing.

"Why didn't you come out when I called you?" Lila asked. "I called and called."

"It was hide-and-seek," Jeffrey responded simply.

Suddenly, Lila turned extremely pale. The shock of the experience was taking its toll. "I think I'm going to faint," she murmured. "My head is pounding…"

Colleen lifted Jeffrey out of Lila's lap and Ted placed her on oxygen. "Nice, slow breaths," he said.

"Blood pressure is 210 over 108," I said. I surmised her blood pressure skyrocketed from the stress.

"Just take some deep breaths and try to relax. Everything is okay now," Barry instructed. "The oxygen will help you feel better."

Since Lila complained of feeling warm, I placed a cool washcloth over the top of her head. "Just sit and rest for a few minutes, and then I'll check your pressure again."

After about ten minutes, Lila said, "I think I'm starting to feel better." A nice pink hue was returning to her cheeks.

"Pressure's now down to 120/84," I said. "Much better."

"Does anyone want to play hide-and-seek with me?" Jeffrey asked hopefully.

"No more hide-and-seek today!" Lila declared.

In the end, Jeffrey was safe and sound and Lila didn't have to go to the hospital. A happy ending to what could have been a disaster. *Thank You, Jesus, for hearing our prayers.*

Choking!

He sent out his word and healed them;
he rescued them from the grave.

PSALM 107:20

A ndrea, help!" my mom cried out.

I rushed downstairs and found my parents in the kitchen. "I think he's choking," Mom said urgently. "Do something! I think he needs the Heimlich maneuver!"

My father leaned against the kitchen counter, trying to cough into the sink. I looked at his face and could see that he was straining to get air in. His bright blue eyes were bulging and he was unable to cough effectively or to speak. I heard a whistling noise and knew it was stridor, a sign of an ineffective airway. Mom was right; Dad needed the Heimlich maneuver right away.

I've been on dozens of choking calls. Usually, by the time I arrive with the ambulance, the patient has already coughed the object out or the police have successfully performed the Heimlich maneuver. Although I've practiced the technique on mannequins and simulated it on other people in our certification courses, I'd never actually performed the technique on a conscious person. Fear threatened to paralyze me...to transfix me to the spot. However, another part of me began to act on an automatic level. Fortunately, my training took precedence over my fear. *Please help me do the right thing, Lord.*

"It's going to be okay, Dad. I'm going to do the Heimlich maneuver on you," I said, trying to keep my voice from shaking. I wrapped my arms around my father's abdomen and placed my hands just above his belly button. I had wrapped my arms around Dad countless times to hug him, but this was so…different. I knew I had to get it right or the unthinkable might happen. The stakes were so high. *We all love you so much, Dad.*

One thrust, two thrusts…Dad began to cough violently. Suddenly, two almonds popped out of his mouth and into the kitchen sink. I heard him begin to suck air deeply into his lungs. Then I reminded *myself* to breathe. I said a silent prayer of thanks. My father, my world, was going to be okay.

"Andrea, I think you'd better call for an ambulance to come over. I think he should go to the hospital and get checked out," Mom said. "What do you think?"

"I think that's a really good idea," I replied. I still felt emotional; I was afraid I wouldn't be able to get the words out when I called the police department. As my mom requested, I dialed 911. I reflected that just a few minutes earlier, I had called upon the "God of the 911." That is, I had said a prayer to the Lord to help me and my family. As far as I know, my campus minister at college coined this phrase. He explained that we call upon God during emergencies, such as when we need assistance during a difficult exam or we ask for help in a time of crisis. His point was that we should remember to thank God and give praise when the emergency is over. We should keep up a daily dialogue with Jesus and not just call out for help when the going gets tough. *Thank You, God, for helping my family today!*

The next thing I knew, my first-aid pager was going off for my own address! A minute after I called 911, Sergeant Flint arrived, followed shortly by my fellow EMS volunteers. It was wonderful to see their friendly, concerned faces.

"I really think I'm okay now. I don't think I need to go to the hospital," Dad protested. Naturally, Mom overruled him.

"Mom will worry until you get a clean bill of health," I said. "You might as well just go now and get it over with."

"You make a good point," Dad said, winking at Mom. Now I knew he *really was* feeling better.

As we drove to the hospital, I reflected on how grateful I was for the support and assistance of my fellow volunteers. Squad members routinely join together to help members of our communities. One thing I have learned during my years on the rescue squad is that we also join together to help each other. We are family.

. . . .

Gary and I took a brief rest from scrubbing the ambulance. "That save this morning was amazing. I can't believe how fast he came back!" Gary exclaimed.

"It was so awesome," Flynn agreed. "The way that guy just popped up like that after the medic zapped him! It was so cool the way he was totally fine, just like that!"

The save *was* pretty amazing, I had to admit. The gentleman, a 52-year-old named Hal McHugh, crossed the finish line of our town's three-mile fall harvest run and immediately went into cardiac arrest. Fortunately for Hal, a cardiologist, a pair of medics, and our entire first aid squad was within spitting distance. The paramedics immediately defibrillated him and in less than thirty seconds, Hal popped up and asked, "What just happened?"

Now, two hours later, we were about half done cleaning our ambulance when our pagers went off.

DISPATCHER: "Request for first aid at the Coastal Cove Restaurant for a choking victim."

The three of us jumped into the ambulance and drove straight to the scene. The Coastal Cove is a beautiful upscale restaurant overlooking a scenic park. One of the valets directed us to park in an open parking space near the front door. "She's in the main lobby," he said.

We met Officer McGovern in the lobby. "The patient's name is Millie Schneider," he said. "She's 96. Her friend said that she started choking and took off for the ladies room. As you can see, she didn't quite make it there. A bystander did the Heimlich maneuver and removed two large shrimp from her mouth. She didn't have a pulse, so we started CPR."

Millie lay flat on her back on the plush carpeted floor. She had a pale, wrinkled face and wore a long plaid skirt with strappy white sandals. Although the shrimp were out, Millie still wasn't breathing. I supposed that she had been without oxygen for too long and that her 96-year-old heart had given out from the stress.

At that time, the standard of care was to perform a precordial thump prior to applying the defibrillator. To perform a precordial thump, one makes a fist and performs a calculated strike to the victim's chest. Back then, precordial thumps were performed by EMTs in cases of witnessed arrest only. They are designed to deliver about two to five joules of energy to a person's heart, as opposed to the 200 to 360 joules provided by a defibrillator. Due to their controversial nature, EMTs no longer perform precordial thumps in our region. I felt nervous about thumping such a frail, elderly woman in the chest. *What if I cause more harm than good?* I pictured her ribs collapsing like a house of cards. "Gary," I whispered, "I'm afraid I'm going to hurt her."

"Better you than me. Anyway, the police have already been doing CPR on her. If her ribs were going to break, they probably already did," he said.

"Well, okay. Here goes…" *Dear Lord, please don't let me hurt her while I am actually trying to help her.* Without further delay, I took a deep breath, made a fist, and gave a single blow to the middle of Millie's sternum.

Gary checked Millie's pulse. "Wow—I think the thump actually worked! She has a strong carotid," he said.

"A decent radial pulse too," Officer McGovern added.

I breathed a huge sigh of relief. Not only had the precordial thump worked, but I felt pretty sure I hadn't broken any of Millie's ribs in the process. Millie began to stir. She coughed the oral airway that had been inserted out of her mouth. She even looked like she was trying to open her eyes. "Hey, her gag reflex is back. That's a good sign too," I said. *Things are definitely starting to look up for Millie Schneider!*

We transported Millie to Bakersville Hospital. I hoped that the event wasn't too much for her body to recover from. If she was without oxygen for too long, she could certainly have brain damage.

Two days later, while on my lunch break working as a physical therapist at the hospital, I decided to go visit Millie. I learned that she was on a general medical floor as opposed to the telemetry floor. I thought that was a pretty good sign. As I entered Millie's room, I could scarcely believe my eyes! Millie was sitting in a high-backed chair working on a crossword puzzle. I suddenly felt choked up. Although Millie was 96, it hadn't been "her time." She was obviously still able to get enjoyment from life.

"Oh, hello," Millie said, looking up. "What can I do for you?"

"I just dropped in to say hello." I explained that I was with her at the Coastal Cove Restaurant, along with my first aid squad.

"I was celebrating a friend's birthday until those shrimp almost did me in! I'm so glad to be alive," she said. "My guardian angel must have been looking out for me."

I gave her a hug. "I'm really glad you're okay."

The next day, I decided to try to visit Hal, the gentleman who we resuscitated at the race. "He's allowed visitors," his nurse said with a smile. "Go right in."

Similarly to Millie, I found Hal sitting up in a chair. He put down his magazine when I entered the room. I explained who I was and why I was visiting.

"I'm so delighted that you came. Please tell me all about it," he exclaimed. "I've been so curious. I don't remember much of anything from that morning. I remember starting the race, but I honestly don't remember anything after the second mile or so."

"Well, let me say that you picked the perfect place to go down—just past the finish line and with EMS personnel all around you. A cardiologist was running next to you and saw you collapse. You had a dozen people working on you within seconds."

Hal chuckled. "That sounds like good planning on my part. And at least I finished the race."

"Are you feeling better?" I noticed that he had an assortment of IV lines, a pulse oximeter, oxygen, and a heart monitor.

"I had an emergency cardiac catheterization that showed numerous blockages. I'm going for heart surgery tomorrow. I guess I'm a pretty lucky guy that I'm even sitting here at all right now. " He grabbed hold of my hand and squeezed it. "Please say a prayer for me."

"I will definitely do that," I promised. "And since I'm a therapist here, I'll see you after your surgery and make sure you start walking and exercising."

Hal sailed through his surgery without complications and made a full recovery. Many years have passed, and Hal is still running!

Our squad assisted with two saves within a few hours of each other on that special day. A day that makes all the hours of training worthwhile, allowing us to serve as healing instruments of Jesus.

Hunting for a Cure

*The human spirit can endure in sickness, but
a crushed spirit who can bear?*

PROVERBS 18:14

Oh no, not again. Sam's cheeks flushed with frustration. He was on his kitchen floor. *Again.* It was getting harder and harder for him to get up. His mother was getting too old and frail to keep pulling him up. She was increasingly relying on the police department and first aid squad to pick him and his brother, Seth, off the floor after they fell.

Why me, Lord? I've always been a nice guy. I've never intentionally hurt anybody. I've always minded my own business and helped others when I could. And now I couldn't help someone even if I wanted to. I can't even help myself.

Slowly, Sam inched his way closer to a kitchen chair. *Maybe if I could just pull myself up onto it, I could somehow spin around and sit down.* Sam tried unsuccessfully to control the tremors in his arms and legs. Each time he reached for the chair, his arm shook so violently that he couldn't seem to grab on and keep hold.

Sam shook his head in disgust. *Look at me. I'm only 42 years old, for crying out loud. I can't even get myself off the floor.* He glanced at his watch. His mother and brother wouldn't be home for another half hour. He decided to rest on the floor for a few moments and then try again.

Sam's mind drifted to his father. *Oh Dad, now I know exactly what you went through.* Sam's father, Edward Winters, had been a successful salesman for a medical equipment company for thirty years. Then, one day, his arm started to tremor. Gradually, it spread to the rest of his body. For years, his entire body would be consumed with constant, thrashing movements. Countless times, he, Seth, and his mother would pick their father up off this very kitchen floor. Eventually, it got so bad that his father had to stay in a wheelchair. Sometimes he would even fall out of that. After years of terrible suffering, Edward Winters finally passed away. *Look at me, Dad. I'm becoming you.*

Sam tried once more to get himself up onto the chair, but his arms and legs refused to cooperate. *Dear Lord, will someone come up with a cure for Huntington's disease before I die from it? Before Seth dies from it? Please, please help us.*

Sam heard footsteps on the porch and was relieved that his mother was home. Relieved, but at the same time embarrassed and ashamed. He dreaded the look of pain and anxiety that he knew he would see in her eyes any second.

"Sam, we're home," Chloe Winters called out. "Where are you?"

"I'm in here, Mom," Sam said softly. He knew his mother worried about leaving him alone. This latest fall would just make her worry more.

"Oh my goodness, Sam, are you okay?" Chloe asked, bending down next to him. "Did you get hurt?"

"No, Mom, I'm okay. It's just that I can't seem to get myself into the chair," he admitted. "Maybe if you could just give me a tiny boost."

"Of course," Chloe said. "Now Seth, you just stay right where you are. Please don't try to help. I don't want you to fall too." Chloe put down her cane and used both hands to try to push Sam from behind.

"Just a little harder, Mom. I think I can do it this time," Sam said hopefully.

Chloe tried several more times, but finally said, "I'm sorry, Sam. I'm just not strong enough anymore. I think I'm going to call the police department. They can give us a hand."

Sam nodded his head. He knew the routine. *If only someone could discover a cure…*

....

DISPATCHER: "Request for first aid at 618 Crestview Drive for a forty-two-year-old fall victim."

"Weren't you just at that house last week?" my mom asked.

"Yes, we go there pretty much every week. There are two brothers who live there with their mother. They tend to fall a lot." I had already responded to their home at least a dozen times. Sometimes the calls were for Seth Winters, who was forty-five. Other times, the calls were for Seth's younger brother, Sam. Seth and Sam had Huntington's disease, also known as Huntington's chorea. Huntington's disease is a genetic disorder. It is a progressive disease best known for uncontrollable "dance-like" writhing movements of the arms and legs ("chorea"). After several torturous years, the disease inevitably results in death.

There is a test people can take for the disease, but unfortunately there is a high suicide rate among those who find out they test positive. Needless to say, the test is controversial.

Mason, Meg, Ted, and I responded to the call. "I wonder if it's for Seth or Sam," Meg said.

"Sam," I answered. "The dispatcher said the call is for a forty-two-year-old. Seth is forty-five."

"Oh, I didn't catch that," Meg said. "What a terrible shame for these two men. These calls always make me feel down."

Our rig pulled up in front of a small blue cottage with yellow trim. Mrs. Winters met us at the front door. She was an older woman with long gray hair which she wore up in a loose bun. "Thanks for coming out again," she said. "I hope we aren't becoming a bother. It's just that I couldn't get Sam up…"

"Please don't feel that way," Mason said. "You're never a bother. That's what we're here for."

"Well, thanks, if you say so," she said, slowly nodding her head. In the past, Mrs. Winters had mentioned that her husband passed away several years earlier from Huntington's disease. I couldn't even imagine what she was going through. First to lose your husband to a rare and fatal disease and then to become the caretaker to your two grown sons, knowing that you would lose them too. It seemed almost unbearable.

I knew it must have been devastating for Seth and Sam when they developed Huntington's chorea. They had seen their father suffer first-hand, so they knew what was in store for them. Sam, a kind and gentle soul, always smiled pleasantly at us. Against all odds, he always maintained hope. Seth, on the other hand, often scowled at us. I didn't take it personally; I realized that the scowls were born of frustration.

Seth was always upset to see us. Even though we weren't there to treat him this time, I think just the sight of us probably sparked unhappy memories. Seth *despised* falling and he was mortified when we had to pick him up off the floor. "I'm fine, I don't need any help!" he would say gruffly. But of course, he wasn't fine and he did need help. *Slowly losing your independence must be brutal.* It was a terrible blow to Seth's pride whenever he needed our help getting up off the floor. Luckily, he usually didn't get hurt from the falls and so didn't have to go to the hospital.

"Does anything hurt, Sam?" Mason asked, kneeling down next to him.

"No, I didn't go down hard," Sam answered. "I just need a hand to get up." I knew it cost him his pride to admit it.

Mason and Ted boosted Sam to his feet and then helped him turn and take a seat in a kitchen chair. It was almost painful to see the way his arms and legs moved uncontrollably. "I'm okay," he said. "Thanks— I don't need to go to the hospital or anything."

As the months passed, Seth's and Sam's falls became more and more frequent. Now, our squad was responding to their home two or three days each week. One night, we were called to help both brothers. "Seth lost his balance," Mrs. Winters explained. "Sam tried to catch him, but Seth ended up taking him down too."

By coincidence, I became Sam's outpatient physical therapist. A coworker, Sophie, treated Seth at the same time. Their physician hoped that physical therapy might improve their strength and balance and decrease their falls. Between the first aid calls and physical therapy sessions, I got to know both of the brothers pretty well.

Sam was absolutely devoted to his physical therapy. He performed all his exercises to the best of his ability, and never once complained that he was tired or that something was too difficult. I admired his strength of spirit and quiet determination. Sam was always willing to try, no matter how daunting the task might seem.

Each week, Sam brought me the latest research articles about Huntington's disease. During each session, Sam would look me right in the eye and ask, "Do you think they'll come up with a cure for Huntington's before I die?"

I dreaded that question. It never failed to make me feel absolutely terrible. "I know they have lots of great scientists working on it," I would say, trying to sound positive. However, I knew the odds weren't good. *Why do the research wheels move so slowly?* I knew Mr. Winters had already succumbed to the disease. I grew worried that it wouldn't be long before Seth and Sam joined their father.

"What if they don't come up with a cure in time for Seth and me?" he would ask. It was a rhetorical question, of course. I would squeeze his shoulder and say, "Well, let's hope that isn't the case." I wanted to strike a balance between staying positive and optimistic, but at the same time not raising false hopes.

Seth passed away first. Toward the end, he could no longer speak or swallow and required total care from his mother. Sam watched from the sidelines, knowing he would be next. As it turned out, he didn't have to wait very long. About six months later, he passed away quietly in his sleep. *Finally, his suffering is over.*

It's years later, and there still isn't a cure for Huntington's disease. And sadly, as far as I know, there is none in sight. To this day, I am haunted by Sam's question: "Do you think they'll come up with a cure for Huntington's before I die?"

In the Blink of an Eye

But you, God, see the trouble of the afflicted; you consider their grief and take it in hand. The victims commit themselves to you; you are the helper of the fatherless.

PSALM 10:14

It was a warm Tuesday evening in early May. Showers earlier in the day had given way to hazy sunshine. The air, now thick with humidity, hinted that summer was not all that far away. My mother and I were in our backyard, engaged in the ongoing battle against some very persistent weeds that seemed determined to infiltrate our flower garden.

DISPATCHER: "Request for first aid at 917 Jefferson Avenue for a motor vehicle accident with possible entrapment."

"That's odd," my mom commented. "The car accident is at a house and not at an intersection."

I quickly stood up and brushed some dirt off my hands and knees. "Yes, maybe the person was pulling out of the driveway or something," I said.

"Well, you'd better hurry. It doesn't sound good. I'll see you in a bit," Mom said. "We're just about done, anyway."

I met up with Mason Chapman and Buddy at the first aid building. Mason notified the dispatcher that we were in service and we took off with lights and sirens to Jefferson Avenue.

"Could be because the roads are still wet from all the rain earlier," Buddy offered. "Is the fire department coming to help with extrication?"

"The dispatcher said they weren't needed. I guess we'll have to see when we get there," Mason replied.

We pulled up in front of house number 917. At first I didn't see anything at all…and then I realized the call was in the driveway of the home and not the street. I was puzzled. "Someone got in a car accident in their own driveway with entrapment?" Some of our calls definitely don't fall into the norm. This call was already sending off red flags that it was going to fall into this category.

I stepped out the back door of the ambulance and looked to my left. Daffodils the color of rich, creamy butter lined a steep gravel driveway. A small red brick house with blue shutters sat at the top of the driveway. A beige, beat-up looking Chevy stood midway up the drive. Officer Endicott was crouched down next to the rear of the car. It looked like someone was stuck under the rear tire, but I couldn't tell for sure from the roadway. I grabbed our first aid kit and hastened to get a better look. Sure enough, when I got closer, I could see that a woman who looked to be about 60 years old was wedged beneath the rear tire.

"This is Bertha Bender," Officer Endicott introduced her while holding stabilization on her head and neck.

"Can I have a cigarette?" Bertha asked. Her words were slurred and her eyes were only half-open.

Intoxicated or head-injury? As I knelt down next to Bertha, I could smell the stench of alcohol on her breath and even emanating from her pores. *Possibly just intoxicated, but better to err on the side of caution.* Bertha's shorts and T-shirt didn't afford her much protection, and I noted that she had numerous abrasions on her arms and legs.

"What happened?" Mason asked, as he silently pointed to me to take over stabilizing Bertha's cervical spine to free up Officer Endicott.

"Someone done gone and ran me over," Bertha said. "Can't you see?"

"I don't see anybody," Buddy said. "But we're going to get you on a backboard and take you to the hospital to get checked out."

"DON'T WANT THE HOSPITAL!" Bertha bellowed. "Can't you people hear? I said I wanted a cigarette. Does the word *hospital* sound like the word *cigarette*? It don't to me. Now just get me up so I can go inside."

"So, who was driving?" Mason whispered to Officer Endicott.

"She was," he said, hiding a smile.

"What?" I asked. "Did you just say Bertha was driving?"

Officer Endicott's eyes twinkled. "Yes, she was. You can't make this stuff up."

We weren't exactly sure how Bertha managed to do it, but we surmised that she wanted to get something out of her trunk and left her car in neutral. As she leaned into her trunk, her car started rolling and knocked her over, pinning her beneath the rear wheel. *She's fortunate that she wasn't more seriously injured. And very lucky that she didn't actually go driving in her condition, since she could have ended up hurting someone else.*

"Help me up," she yelled, shoving my hands off her head and squirming her way out from under the tire. "I said I need a cigarette. And a beer!"

We cleansed and bandaged Bertha's abrasions. Since she was alert and oriented, we allowed her to sign a refusal form to decline transportation to the hospital. It appeared that the only thing truly hurt was her pride.

"If you don't feel well later, you can always change your mind and call us back," I said to her. This is one of our standard lines when someone signs a refusal.

"Sure, when pigs fly, I'll do that," Bertha muttered as she walked toward her front door.

"I can really feel the love on this call," Mason remarked sarcastically. "I feel so appreciated."

"I can feel it too," Buddy smiled, picking up some empty bandage wrappers from Bertha's driveway.

The world of volunteer EMS can be funny. Sometimes people appreciate what we do, and in other instances, they don't. Either way, it's okay. Most of us aren't doing this in order to be appreciated.

....

DISPATCHER: "Request for first aid at 48 Bartholomew Road for a woman with leg pain."

Honestly, what I really wanted to do was put my pillow over my head in a desperate attempt to block out the sound of my pager. I was feeling more tired than usual and was looking forward to an uninterrupted night's sleep. *But I guess it's not to be.* Almost reluctantly, I climbed out of bed, slipped on my sneakers, and popped a piece of spearmint gum in my mouth.

I was glad to see that Archie was already in the driver's seat when I arrived at the building. I prefer to be in the back with the patient anyway, and I was still feeling a bit too sleepy to be driving. Gary sat in the front seat, next to Archie. "Girl, you look like you need some more sleep," he called back to me.

"Thanks," I grumbled. "I was working on it when the call went off." I knew his ribbing was good-natured. *I probably should have run a brush through my hair though.* I tried to run my fingers through it to neaten it up a bit, figuring that would make me look slightly less bed-rumpled and hopefully a little bit more presentable.

We pulled up in front of a stately colonial overlooking the Atlantic. Numerous balconies on the second and third floors were carefully designed to maximize the ocean views. Outdoor lighting drew attention to an impressive rock garden.

Officer Endicott met us out by the ambulance. "Hate to break the news to you," he began, "but the Cook family is absolutely determined that you take the patient to Montgomery Hospital. They say they know someone on the board of trustees there."

"But we never go that far away," Archie protested. "That's way out of our response area. And anyway, it's not a good idea in the summer. I don't want to take a rig out of the service area for so long. What if we have another call?"

"It's not me you have to convince. It's the Cooks," Officer Endicott said. "I tried to explain all that to them already, but they'd hear nothing of it."

My heart sank. Normally, our squad goes to one of two hospitals, each of which is approximately 15 minutes away. I'd never been to Montgomery Hospital, but I knew it was a solid 45 minute drive. *At this rate, I'll never catch up on sleep.*

"Let's go in and try to change their minds," Gary said, leading the way.

Ashley Cook sat in an elegant French cane side chair in the dining room. I thought she looked about 60 years old or so. She tucked a strand of long brownish-gray hair behind her left ear and puckered her brow. "My left leg has been hurting for the past few days," she explained. "I decided perhaps I should go get it checked out, since I had a stroke two years ago. My husband could drive me, of course, but I think I'll get faster service if I arrive by ambulance."

Mrs. Cook stated a common misconception. People sometimes call us for transportation because they think they'll get seen by a doctor more quickly if they arrive by ambulance. In reality, the triage nurse will evaluate them and determine how quickly they should be seen with respect to the extent of their illness or injury. It's pointless to try to explain this to people because they never seem to believe us. *I guess it's something one has to figure out on his or her own. And if Mrs. Cook is truly "friends with someone on the board," perhaps she'll be seen more quickly after all.*

Archie tried his best to explain to the Cook family all the reasons that we would prefer to take Mrs. Cook to Bakersville Hospital. "It ties up our members as well as our resources," he finished.

The Cooks wouldn't budge. After a while, we grew to realize that in the time it would take to convince the Cooks to go to the local hospital, we could have already driven them to Montgomery Hospital. "I guess we should make an exception and accommodate her wishes, or we'll be here all night," Archie grunted to Gary and me. We nodded in agreement.

The trip to Montgomery Hospital was uneventful, and it was close to midnight when we were finally on our way home. "Do you want to sit up front with Archie?" Gary asked.

"No thanks," I replied. "I'm going to lie down and try to catch some

Z's." I strapped a seatbelt around my waist and then curled up on my side on the bench in the rear of the ambulance. Although it was difficult to get comfortable, within five minutes or so I drifted into a light sleep.

I awoke with a start when Archie hollered, "Look out!" and slammed on the breaks. I heard squealing tires followed by a loud bang. As my adrenalin began surging, I tried to get my bearings and leaned forward to look out the front window of the ambulance. *What is going on? Did we just get hit? It didn't feel like we did, but it sure did sound like we did!*

Two cars, one going northbound and one going eastbound, had collided at a major intersection directly in front of our ambulance. Both looked as though they had sustained significant damage. The passenger side of an old, beat-up black sedan was smashed in and the front end of a green SUV was severely crumpled.

Archie quickly flipped on our ambulance lights to protect us from getting hit ourselves. "I'm going to call this in to headquarters, and then I'll help you out," Archie said, as he picked up the radio handset. "We need police and first aid at the intersection of 39 and 43 for a motor vehicle accident. Unknown injuries at this time."

"Let's see what we've got," Gary said. "Can you get me a pair of gloves?"

"A difference of a few seconds and it could have been us," I said, tossing a pair of gloves up front to him. I grabbed the first aid kit and a large orange flashlight before exiting out the side door.

"Why don't I check the SUV and you can check the sedan?" Gary suggested.

"Sounds good," I agreed, and jogged over to the sedan, careful to avoid broken glass and a piece of a fender. As I approached the car, I could hear a woman sobbing. I tapped on her window and then carefully opened the driver's side door. The woman's long dark hair obscured much of her face. She clutched one of her hands with the other, and from a glance, it looked like an obvious compound open fracture of her wrist. *No wonder she's sobbing.* A young boy, about ten years of age with short dark hair, sat in the passenger seat next to her. He was moaning and holding his right hand over his right eye. Although it was dark, I could see that blood was slowly trickling down his right cheek.

"How are you doing?" I asked. "What are your names? Please tell me what's hurting you."

"Rosa Diaz," the woman said softly. "Manny Diaz," she added, pointing to the boy. "*No Ingles*," she said, shaking her head.

Unfortunately, my Spanish is extremely limited. "*Dolor?*" I asked, which means "Pain?"

"*Mucho*," Rosa said, pointing to her left wrist.

"*Mucho*," Manny said, pointing to his right eye.

I crossed around to the other side of the car. I knew I needed to get a better look at what was going on with Manny's eye.

"What ya got?" Archie asked, coming up beside me.

I pointed to Rosa. "Can you assess her please? I got as far as the injured wrist and I was about to take a closer look at the boy."

Archie didn't speak Spanish either, but he tried his best with hand gestures and the few Spanish words that he knew to communicate with Rosa. I was now free to focus my attention on Manny. "Can you let me see your eye?" I asked, pointing toward his eye so that he would better understand what I wanted.

Briefly, he lowered his right hand and I used a flashlight to take a look. *Something is definitely not right here. His eyeball looks intact, but something is missing. Oh—it's his eyelid! His eyelid is gone! What in the world does a doctor do for a severed eyelid? Is that even replaceable?*

I quickly checked the quality of his pulse; it was strong and steady. I could hear sirens in the distance and knew that the police would be arriving shortly. Although Manny wasn't complaining of neck pain, I was pretty sure that he hadn't been wearing a seatbelt at the time of the crash. Given the way his car looked and to be on the safe side, I decided to climb into the rear of the car and hold his head still to immobilize his cervical spine. Once help arrived, I figured either myself or another EMT could do a more detailed head-to-toe assessment.

Within a minute, a young police officer stood beside me. "Hi, I'm Officer Hendricks. What's going on?" he asked, holding a small notepad in his hand.

I gave him a brief rundown of what we had witnessed. "And I think his eyelid was torn off," I added.

He grabbed hold of my flashlight and carefully examined the front passenger side of the car. "I think I found it!" he declared. There, wedged in the slit of the glove compartment, was Manny's eyelid! Slowly and carefully, Officer Hendricks extricated the eyelid and placed it in moist sterile gauze. Moments later, the volunteer first aid squad arrived and we helped them get the three patients ready for transport to the hospital.

Just before we lifted Manny into an ambulance, I squeezed his hand. "Good luck," I said. "I'll be thinking of you." I wasn't sure if he understood me, but I think he got the general idea. I said a quick silent prayer that the surgeons would be able to successfully reattach Manny's eyelid.

Archie, Gary, and I climbed back into the ambulance and once more headed for home. This time, however, I found that I wasn't sleepy anymore. *Thank goodness the accident occurred after we had already dropped Mrs. Cook off at the hospital.*

We found out two days later that a plastic surgeon successfully reattached Manny's eyelid. Rosa was diagnosed with a fractured wrist and a sprained ankle and made a full recovery.

A Little Dose of Sugar

*But let all who take refuge in you be glad; let them
ever sing for joy. Spread your protection over them,
that those who love your name may rejoice in you.*

PSALM 5:11

ianna Lee felt herself break out into a cold sweat. She knew the feeling all too well. *Did I eat lunch today? I'd better get to the kitchen and get some peanut butter crackers.* Gianna tried to stand up from her desk chair, but her legs felt shaky. *Maybe I should sit for a minute first. I wonder if Mom's home. Maybe I can just call her and she'll bring me something to eat.*

Gianna tried to stand up again, but her legs buckled and she sat down hard on the edge of her bed, right next to her desk. *Did I take my insulin today? It gets so confusing to keep track of it all.* "Mom?" Gianna tried to call out, but her voice sounded weak and funny to her own ears. *This is not good. My hands and feet are tingling, and my mind feels so fuzzy.*

Once more, Gianna tried once to stand up, but instead fell backward onto her bed. *Let me just close my eyes for a minute, and I'll feel better. Then I can get something to eat.* Despite her intentions, Gianna drifted into unconsciousness.

....

> **DISPATCHER:** "Request for first aid at 114 Hudson Avenue for a diabetic emergency."

"Weren't you just there the other day?" my dad asked, overhearing my pager.

"Yes, we've been there quite a lot lately," I answered, grabbing a set of car keys and heading for our back door. I figured the first aid call was for Gianna Lee. According to her mother, Gianna had been diabetic since childhood. Now she was twenty, and she wasn't very good about taking her medication correctly or being careful with her diet.

I met up with Dillon, Helen, Buddy, and Ted at the first aid building. "Good thing we have a nice turnout. Gianna's strong as an ox," Buddy remarked.

"It took five of us to hold her down for the IV last week," Dillon said. Gianna couldn't help it, but she tended to be *extremely* combative when she was having a hypoglycemic episode.

Gianna lived on a lovely street lined with cherry blossom trees. Buddy parked in front of their home and I carried our first aid bag up the all-too-familiar path to Gianna's front door. Gianna's mother met us in the living room. "She's in the bedroom," she said. "Thanks for coming out again. I think she took too much insulin but didn't eat enough lunch, but I'm really not sure," she said. Mrs. Lee was a kind woman who did the best she could for her daughter—and the rest of her family as well. She worked several jobs to make ends meet and always made sure there was enough food on the table.

By the time our squad arrived, Gianna was often in full-blown insulin shock, also referred to as a diabetic coma. Diabetes is a metabolic disease in which the body cannot appropriately control the amount of sugar in the blood because it doesn't have enough insulin. Insulin shock, also known as hypoglycemia or low blood sugar, comes on quickly and can cause confusion and unconsciousness. Diabetic coma, or high blood sugar, occurs gradually over a period of days or weeks. It is marked by thirst, frequent urination, and fatigue. If untreated, diabetic coma can also lead to unconsciousness.

We found Officers Endicott and Sims in the bedroom with Gianna. "We can't give her any oral glucose," Officer Endicott explained. "She's already unconscious." Giving food or sugar to an unconscious patient could cause aspiration into the lungs.

Gianna lay at an odd angle across her bed, as if she had passed out and just happened to land there. I glanced out her bedroom window. "Looks like Baxter and Roberta are coming in right behind us," I said. I knew Gianna would need IV glucose from the paramedics in order to come around.

"Our young friend again, huh?" Baxter asked when he entered the bedroom. "I think we all recall the procedure from last time. Everyone needs to take responsibility for an arm or leg and don't let her pull the IV out," he said as he began prepping the IV line.

Buddy and Dillon each held down one of Gianna's arms while Ted took one of her legs, and Helen and I together held down her other leg. Gianna was incredibly strong, which we had learned the hard way.

Baxter pushed the tube of glucose through the IV. "Gianna should be waking up now any second," he said. As if on cue, Gianna began attempting to open her eyes.

Gianna thrashed and bucked on the bed, but gradually her limbs quieted. Slowly, she opened her eyes and blinked in confusion at seeing so many faces. "Uh-oh," she said sheepishly. "Did I mess up my sugar again?"

"Yes, that about sums it up," Roberta said. "You really need to be more careful. All this bouncing around of your sugar levels really isn't good for you."

"I'll be more careful, I promise," she said. "I'm sorry to bring you all out here again."

I was always startled by the sharp contrast between Gianna when she was an unruly patient with low blood sugar, and how incredibly sweet and polite she was when she regained consciousness. *Thank You, Lord, for helping Gianna again.*

Months passed, and I became Gianna's outpatient physical therapist. She developed a diabetic ulcer on the bottom of her foot, a common complication of diabetes. At that time, standard treatment included whirlpool, debridement with tweezers, and bandaging. Each Monday, Gianna would come in for her physical therapy appointment, and her wound would be encrusted with sand. "Gianna, did you go to the beach again?" I would ask.

Gianna would smile. "Sorry about that, Andrea. There were some good waves…"

"Gianna, if you keep walking barefoot in the sand, it's going to be awfully hard to heal that wound." Gianna would always just smile and nod, and I knew she'd be back at the beach the next day.

....

DISPATCHER: "Request for first aid at 114 Hudson Avenue for an unconscious female."

Here we go again. I hope Gianna's okay. Dillon, Helen, Buddy, and Ted climbed into the ambulance with me.

"Poor girl," Ted remarked. "She seems to have such an awfully difficult time controlling her sugar."

"Yes, we've been coming here for so many years," Helen said. "Too bad she's not a candidate for an insulin pump or something."

As the sun was setting, cherry blossoms tumbled haphazardly down the street in the breeze. Once more I followed the familiar stone pathway to Gianna's front door.

I could tell right away that this call was different from all the past ones. Mrs. Lee met us at the front door as usual, but this time she was crying. "I don't think my baby's breathing," she sobbed. "She's down the hall in her bedroom."

We raced along the hall toward Gianna's bedroom. Officers Endicott and Sims had already pulled Gianna off the bed and placed her on the hardwood floor. "No pulse," Officer Sims said tersely. "We're hooking up the defibrillator right now."

I stared for a brief second in shock before I sprang into action. *I cannot believe this is happening. I cannot believe Gianna is gone!* I had met Gianna so many times first as a squad member and then later as her physical therapist that I thought of her more as a friend than as a patient. I glanced up at the cross over Gianna's bed. *I'm glad Gianna's not alone.*

Helen hooked up the defibrillator, placing the defibrillator pads on her right upper and left lower chest. "All clear," she said, waving her arm over Gianna's body to ensure our safety.

"No shock advised," the unit said. "Continue CPR."

We worked for several minutes, mostly in silence, each of us deep in our own thoughts.

"Medics are here," Ted said, breaking the silence. "Baxter and Roberta."

The paramedics did everything they could: intubation, IV line, medications. But it was no use. Our friend Gianna was gone.

. . . .

About 19 or 20 years passed before I responded to another call at the Lees' home. I recognized Gianna's mother right away. She had more wrinkles and more gray hair, but she still had the same kind eyes and gentle manner. "It's my aunt," she said. "She's having some stomach pain."

I took hold of her hand. "I still think of Gianna," I said.

"Me too," she said, her eyes growing misty. "Each and every day."

I hadn't meant to upset Mrs. Lee, but I wanted her to know that I remembered Gianna (in a good way). If I close my eyes, I can picture her so vividly: the lean arms and legs, the long, curly hair, and the quick smile. Sometimes, when you have a patient so many times and she always gets better with a little dose of sugar, it's truly hard to believe she's actually gone. Gianna touched each of us in a special way during her short time on this earth. I feel privileged that I had a chance to know her.

Saving Mr. O'Leary

*At sunset, the people brought to Jesus all who
had various kinds of sickness, and laying his
hands on each one, he healed them.*

LUKE 4:40

Jason O'Leary took off his sunglasses and wiped a speck of sand out of his eyes. He couldn't keep up with his wife on their daily morning walk on the boardwalk anymore like he used to, but it was okay. *I appreciate the gift of this beautiful day.*

He thought about taking a rest on a bench for a few minutes, but changed his mind and walked on. He planned to walk a mile and didn't want to keep his wife waiting. She usually walked two miles in the time he walked one. The couple had been married for well over 50 years, but just in the last year he found it was getting a bit harder to keep up with his wife.

Jason felt more tired than usual this morning. *Maybe I should rest for a little bit after all.* He wished he hadn't forgotten his water bottle at home. He felt as though he could really use a nice cool drink.

Jason spotted the next bench. It was only about ten yards away. *Piece of cake...I can make it there.* But suddenly, Jason found himself wondering if he *could* make it there. His legs simply didn't want to cooperate anymore. He felt himself breaking out into a cold sweat and his chest started to feel heavy. Very, very heavy.

Jason felt his legs getting slower and slower. *That's funny. The sun doesn't seem so bright anymore.* Jason felt himself sink slowly down to his knees. *What's happening to me?* Jason never felt himself hit the boardwalk, for his heart had stopped beating. Jason O'Leary was in cardiac arrest.

A retired firefighter happened to be jogging by at that exact moment and witnessed Mr. O'Leary's collapse. He quickly knelt down next to him and felt for a pulse. Finding none, he immediately began to perform CPR.

"Listen," the officer said to a woman who was walking by. "This man needs help! Run to the beach office and call for an ambulance. Tell them that CPR is in progress!"

....

It was a Tuesday in early June and I happened to have the day off. I planned to sleep late and then head to the beach with friends. As is often the case, I got up unexpectedly a little earlier than I planned to when my pager went off.

> **DISPATCHER:** "Request for first aid at the Chestnut Street Boardwalk for an unresponsive male."

I yanked on a pair of shorts and put in my contact lenses with lightning speed. A minute later, I was hopping into the back of the ambulance with Gary.

> **DISPATCHER:** "Update: bystander CPR in progress."

"I knew it," Gary said. "It's going to be one of those days." He grabbed the defibrillator and prepared for the call by opening a package of electrodes. "It'll save time if I hook these up now."

"Good idea." Every minute was precious; we both knew our patient needed rapid defibrillation to have a decent chance of survival. Holding on to an overhead railing with one hand to keep my balance, I grabbed our suction unit and airway kit from an overhead cabinet.

"Something's wrong!" Gary exclaimed. "There's something jammed in the port. I can't attach the electrodes. It looks like a piece of electrode from the last CPR call must have broken off and gotten wedged in."

"Gary, that's horrible! What are we going to do? Are you sure you can't get it off?" Without that defibrillator, our patient's chances of survival would drop dramatically. Our frustration levels skyrocketed. At that time, police departments in our area were not yet carrying defibrillators.

As we pulled up to the scene, Gary looked out our rear window. "I see Buddy pulling up in his car. I'm going to send him back to the building to get the other defibrillator."

With that, Gary jumped out and flagged down Buddy. Buddy didn't have to be told twice. He threw his car in reverse and headed back toward the building. *But it will delay defibrillation by at least six or eight minutes. The golden window will be long over. By then, our patient may have anoxic brain damage!*

The broken defibrillator was lying on the bench in the back of the ambulance. Suddenly, inspiration struck. I grabbed the defibrillator and shoved the broken-off piece of electrode cable into my mouth! A metallic taste assaulted my senses, but I ignored it. I tried not to think about the fact that the piece of metal I was gnawing on had recently been attached to a dead person. Clamping the tiny piece of metal between my molars, I pulled for all I was worth.

For a few long seconds...nothing. Then—bang! The piece of metal broke loose and I spat it out on the floor. Operation "fix the defibrillator with my teeth" was a success and all my teeth were still intact! Holding the defibrillator with one hand, I quickly gathered up our other equipment and hurried along the path that wound through the dunes and up to the boardwalk.

It wasn't hard to find our patient. He was the one in the middle of a large circle of bystanders. I thrust the defibrillator at Gary. "I fixed it," I said without preamble.

He threw me a questioning look.

"Don't ask. It involved my teeth."

Gary nodded and quickly hooked it up to our patient.

Officer McGovern checked our patient's ID cards in his wallet. "He's a local. Name is Jason O'Leary. He's seventy-four years old."

Jason was wearing a white T-shirt, blue nylon running shorts, and sneakers. I figured he must have been out for an early morning walk.

"A retired firefighter started CPR," Officer McGovern added. "Witnessed arrest."

While I performed chest compressions, Mason cut off Mr. O'Leary's T-shirt and Gary applied the electrodes.

"Shock advised," the defibrillator unit announced. Gary pressed the shock button. The unit delivered a stack of three shocks, followed by one additional shock.

I found myself holding my breath and silently saying a prayer. *Dear Lord, please let this work.*

Mason felt along the side of Mr. O'Leary's neck. "He's got a carotid pulse!" he announced. As we strapped Mr. O'Leary onto our backboard, Mason continued to breathe for him with the ambu bag. Although Mr. O'Leary wasn't breathing, I thought his color was improving.

The medics, Ty and Paula, arrived from the hospital. While Paula hooked Mr. O'Leary up to their heart monitor, Ty efficiently intubated him. When they were done, we lifted Mr. O'Leary onto our stretcher. "Good job, everybody. He's in a sinus rhythm," Paula said.

As Mason and Gary rolled the stretcher toward our ambulance, I paused to pick up some of our equipment from the boardwalk. I felt a light tap on my shoulder. "Excuse me," a woman with bright blue eyes and a kind face said. "Are you taking someone to the hospital?"

"Yes," I answered. "Are you missing someone?"

"I think that's my husband," she said. "It was hard to see through the crowd, but I think I saw a peek of his blue shorts."

"What's your husband's name?" I asked.

"Jason O'Leary," she answered.

I put my arm around her shoulders. I wasn't sure why, but Mrs. O'Leary reminded me of my own mother. I suddenly felt choked up and fought it off. "Walk with me," I said. "I'll take you to our ambulance. We're going to bring your husband to Bakersville Hospital. If you like, you can sit in the front seat and ride with us."

"Is he okay?" she whispered, grabbing hold of my hand.

"Well, his heart stopped and an officer who happened to be walking by started CPR." I gauged her facial expression to see if I could keep going. She appeared to be holding up okay, so I continued. "We shocked him four times and got his pulse back. Right now, we are helping him breathe."

"Is Jason going to live?" she asked me, her grip on my hand tightening.

I really wasn't sure how to answer that question. I wasn't sure if he would live or not. He had at least a decent chance, but he could always take a turn for the worse again. In the end, I didn't answer her question directly. "The medics are with him now," I said. "They come from the hospital and give advanced life support. They are giving him medications to help his heart."

"Jason and I walk the boards every day, but I walk faster. I walked ahead like I always do, and on my way back I saw that crowd, and I just knew it was going to be him."

I gave her a hug and helped her into the front seat. "We're doing our best."

"I know you are. Thank you." She blinked away a few tears as I strapped her in.

I hopped into the back. Gary was squeezing the ambu bag once every five seconds while Ty administered medications intravenously. Mason drove the paramedics' rig so that both Ty and Paula could remain in the back of our ambulance.

Gary and I took turns squeezing the ambu bag on the way to the hospital. "You're going to be okay, Mr. O'Leary," I whispered to him. "Your wife is with us in the front seat. I can tell how much she loves you. We're taking you to the hospital." I wasn't sure if Jason could hear me or not. I always like to talk to our patients just in case they can hear. Perhaps they may need a little push, an incentive if you will, to keep holding on. If that's the case, then I want to make sure I provide it.

Mr. O'Leary was admitted to the cardiac critical care unit (CCU). Two days later, Gary and I were at Bakersville Hospital on another first aid call.

"Do you want to run up and see how Mr. O'Leary is doing?" I asked. I had high hopes that he was doing better.

Gary glanced at his watch. "Great idea. I have time."

I had recently graduated from physical therapy school and was now working at Bakersville Hospital. I led the way up to the CCU. We found Mr. O'Leary's nurse, Julie, sitting at the station, working on the computer. I went to high school with Julie. She is smart, knowledgeable, and passionate about her patients. I felt better knowing that Mr. O'Leary was in such capable hands.

"We were hoping you could tell us how Mr. O'Leary is doing," Gary said.

"Not good," Julie said flatly. "We took him off sedation this morning and he became very agitated. He tried to yank his tube out."

My heart sank. "How's his prognosis?" I asked.

"Very poor," Julie said. She picked up a clipboard from the counter and then glanced over at Mr. O'Leary's room. "Very poor," she repeated.

My heart sank further. I peeked through the curtain at him. Mr. O'Leary was sedated and his eyes were closed. He was still intubated and a ventilator breathed for him. I bit back a strong wave of disappointment. My mind wandered to his sweet wife. *I don't want her to be alone; she would be devastated without her husband.* I don't know why, but I had really thought he was going to be okay. Now I had to accept that he might never leave the hospital after all.

....

Two days later

"Hello, is this Jerome Franklin?"

"Yes, this is Dispatcher Franklin with the Pine Cove Police Department. How can I help you?"

"This is Mrs. Boone," she said.

"Hi, Mrs. Boone. I hope you're well tonight. What can I do for you?"

"Jerome, I'm starting to have chest pains. I know something isn't quite right with me. Could you please call an ambulance for me? I think I'd better go to the hospital."

Mrs. Boone, a retired nurse in her eighties, had lived in Pine Cove her entire life. Her father had been a police officer in town for many years, so she felt a special kinship with the police department. She made it a point to keep up-to-date with their names and faces.

"Mrs. Boone, I'm going to send the police and an ambulance right away. Just sit tight and they will be there momentarily," he advised her. "Is your front door unlocked?"

"Yes, I'm pretty sure it is," she answered.

"Okay, hold on just one moment. I'm going to dispatch the ambulance now," he said.

> **DISPATCHER:** "Request for first aid at 216 Horizon Avenue for a woman complaining of chest pain."

"Jerome? Are you there? The pain is getting worse."

"Mrs. Boone, I'm right here with you. Please don't hang up. Stay on the line. Our officers should be there within the minute to help you," Jerome said. "Keep talking to me."

Jerome's instructions were met with silence. "Mrs. Boone? Do you hear me?"

When Officers Endicott and Sims knocked on the front door, Mrs. Boone did not answer. Officer Endicott tried the doorknob, and, finding it unlocked, the pair quickly stepped inside.

They found Mrs. Boone sitting in a chair by the front bay window. Her head hung down over her chest. "Mrs. Boone, are you okay?" Officer Endicott said as he rushed toward her. Quickly, he felt for a carotid pulse. "No pulse." The two men carefully lowered her onto the floor and initiated CPR.

Darren, Gary, and I arrived with the ambulance. I hooked up the defibrillator and pressed the analyze button. "Shock advised," the unit said. I knew Mrs. Boone had not been down for very long. *Jesus, please let her be okay!* I pressed the shock button and the defibrillator delivered two shocks.

"She's got a weak pulse," Gary said, palpating her carotid artery on the right side of her neck. *Now she just has to keep it!*

Unfortunately, Mrs. Boone's heart kept beating only for a minute or two. We started CPR again. *Come on, Mrs. Boone. I know you still have a chance. You were just talking to our dispatcher a couple of minutes ago!*

Paramedics Baxter and Roberta arrived within a few minutes. "We gave her two shocks so far," Gary told them.

Roberta switched to her own defibrillator and shocked Mrs. Boone again. Her frail body jerked in response to the joules of energy that rushed through her.

"I've got a carotid," Baxter said. "Get me a blood pressure and continue with ventilations." Mrs. Boone's blood pressure was 106/54. *Okay, Mrs. Boone, that's a respectable blood pressure. Now, dear Lord, please let her keep it!*

This time, Mrs. Boone's pulse came back to stay. After Baxter intubated her, Gary and I loaded her into the ambulance and Darren took the driver's seat. On the way to the hospital, Roberta continued to administer intravenous medications while Gary continued to breathe for Mrs. Boone with the ambu bag. *So far, so good.*

When we were about halfway to the hospital, Darren, shouted, "Look out the window to your right!" The sight was not a pretty one. One of the paramedics' ambulances lay on its side up against a telephone pole. First aid squad members from a neighboring community were already on the scene and assisting the victims.

I recognized one of the patients being strapped to a backboard; it was Ty, the paramedic who'd helped us resuscitate Mr. O'Leary only four days earlier. How quickly the tables had been turned! Instead of providing emergency care, Ty was now receiving it.

We couldn't stop of course; we had Mrs. Boone, still in critical condition, in the back of our ambulance. All I could do was say a prayer for Ty. I comforted myself that he was already receiving emergency care. But regardless, it's hard to drive by an injured friend.

When we arrived at Harrison Hospital, we learned that a truck had blown a stop sign and struck the medics' rig. The rig subsequently flipped and struck a pole. Ironically, Ty was admitted to the same critical care unit as Mr. O'Leary at Bakersville Hospital.

....

Exactly seven days later, my mom called me at work. "Your man woke up," she said excitedly.

"What? How?" My heart started to race with excitement. I knew she could only be talking about Mr. O'Leary.

"I was swimming at the pool this morning. One of my friends heard that Mr. O'Leary woke up this morning. He's talking and everything," Mom said.

I could barely wait until my lunch hour. When the clock struck twelve, I ran up to the CCU to visit him. "Is it all right if I go in and say hello?" I asked his nurse.

She smiled. "Go right ahead. He's doing fine. I think he'll enjoy the company."

I hesitated at the threshold of the room. Mr. O'Leary was sitting up in bed. He was wearing glasses and reading a newspaper. *He was reading a newspaper!* The ventilator was gone, replaced with a simple nasal oxygen cannula. I was nervous and at the same time overjoyed. It felt almost surreal to visit a person I had helped to resuscitate. How incredibly different he looked!

I took a deep breath, trying to calm the butterflies that were doing a happy dance in my abdomen. I knocked softly on the door. He looked up, smiled, and waved me in.

"Hi, my name is Andrea. I'm a physical therapist here, but I'm also a member of the first aid squad." I paused, not sure what to say next.

"Do you mean you were on the boardwalk with me?" he asked.

"Yes, I was on the boardwalk with you that morning."

"You saved my life. Thank you." His sincerity made every call I have ever answered worthwhile.

"Well, I just helped—there were other first aiders and police too. Luckily, a retired firefighter came by and started CPR."

"Do you know who he is?" Mr. O'Leary asked.

"No, sorry, he left right after we arrived. I never even saw him."

"I don't remember what happened that day. Maybe that's for the best," he joked. I told him a little bit about that morning without going into too much detail. I skipped over the part about me chewing on the defibrillator cables!

"I am so glad you are doing so well," I said, blinking back tears of happiness. "Will you please visit us after you get out of the hospital?"

"I'd love to," he said.

....

The very next day, I found out that Mrs. Boone was also off the ventilator and doing well. And Ty was transferred from the ICU to a step-down unit. Although it would take him numerous weeks, he would go on to make a full recovery!

Mr. O'Leary was true to his word. Six weeks later, Grace O'Leary called me. "We're ready to visit now," she said. "Jason is much stronger." I could practically hear the happiness radiating from her voice. *Thank You, God, for the precious gift of life.*

Mr. O'Leary and his wife stopped by to visit during our business meeting. The sound of his heavy tread as he climbed the stairs to our second floor was like music to my ears. To my knowledge, it was the first time a person we had helped to resuscitate ever came to visit us.

Mr. O'Leary is an example of the healing power of Jesus. Many events came together that morning for a successful outcome. A retired fireman just happened to walk by at the right time and start immediate CPR. I made the spur-of-the-moment decision to chew on the defibrillator port in a last-ditch effort to fix it. As it turned out, the same electrode cable problem was happening to other squads, and so the company that makes them remedied the problem. And so, with the grace of God, the bystanders, police, and EMS all worked together so that Mr. O'Leary could spend another ten years with his wife and family.

Andrea Jo Rodgers has been a volunteer EMT for 26 years and has responded to more than 6500 first-aid and fire calls. She holds a clinical doctorate in physical therapy and has worked as a physical therapist in a trauma center for 20 years.

Angels in the ER

Inspiring True Stories from an Emergency Room Doctor

Twenty-five years in the ER could become a résumé for despair, but for bestselling author Dr. Robert D. Lesslie it's a foundation for inspiring stories of everyday "angels"—friends, nurses, doctors, patients, even strangers who offer love, help, and support in the midst of trouble.

"The ER is a difficult and challenging place to be. Yet the same pressures and stresses that make this place so challenging also provide an opportunity to experience some of life's greatest wonders and mysteries."

Dr. Lesslie illuminates messages of hope while sharing fast-paced, captivating stories about

- discovering lessons from the ER frontline
- watching everyday miracles unfold
- holding onto faith during tragedy and triumph
- embracing the healing balm of hope

If you enjoy true stories of the wonders of the human spirit, this immensely popular book is a reminder that hope can turn emergencies into opportunities and trials into demonstrations of God's grace.

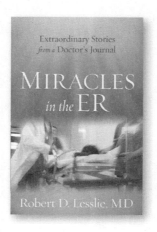

Miracles in the ER
Extraordinary Stories from a Doctor's Journal

You've heard about them. Extraordinary...unexplainable...seemingly miraculous true stories that couldn't have happened—but did. Real-life stories of life changes, answered prayers, inner and outer healing where they appeared impossible.

Again and again, bestselling author Dr. Robert Lesslie has encountered such *Miracles in the ER* during his decades of experience in emergency medicine. In these vignettes—all true stories—Dr. Lesslie chronicles miracles of...

- physical healing
- joy and forgiveness
- restored relationships
- time granted and spent
- angels—human and otherwise

These touching, dramatic, thought-provoking snapshots of life will grace you with hope and prompt you to look more closely for the miracle stories around you that so often go unseen and untold.

To learn more about Harvest House books and
to read sample chapters, visit our website:

www.harvesthousepublishers.com

HARVEST HOUSE PUBLISHERS
EUGENE, OREGON